E S S E N T I A L

MG T SERIES
AND PRE-WAR MIDGETS

ESSENTIAL
MG T SERIES
AND PRE-WAR MIDGETS

THE CARS AND THEIR STORY
1929-55

ANDERS DITLEV CLAUSAGER

SPECIAL PHOTOGRAPHY BY
NEILL BRUCE AND JOHN COLLEY

Published 1995 by Bay View Books Ltd
The Red House, 25-26 Bridgeland Street,
Bideford, Devon EX39 2PZ

© Copyright 1995 by Bay View Books Ltd
Edited by Mark Hughes
Typesetting and design by Chris Fayers & Sarah Ward

ISBN 1 870979 60 5
Printed in Hong Kong

CONTENTS

BIRTH OF THE MIDGET

For more than 70 years the initials MG have been synonymous with sports cars. Despite numerous changes in circumstances the marque has survived where so many other famous British names have fallen by the wayside. There is an enduring magic attached to the cars with the octagonal badge, and although at times it has seemed that MG, too, was doomed to extinction, the marque has staged a comeback and reached new heights of popularity. MG's fame has spread across the world. It became America's favourite sports car, from the time that Edsel Ford of the Ford Motor Company bought an MG in 1930. Hundreds of thousands of MGs followed this first car across the Atlantic.

Edsel Ford's car was an M-type, the first of the MG Midgets. To a later generation the term MG Midget is perhaps mostly connected with those cars made between 1961-79, but the original MG Midgets were made between 1929-55 – and these were the cars that truly founded the MG tradition. The name Midget was aptly chosen for this range of small and affordable sports cars,

yet these Midgets became giant-killers, their reputation bolstered by a formidable series of successes in motor racing and record-breaking. Although MG's heyday in the sport lasted a mere five years, from 1931 to 1935, the legend created by these cars has lived on.

Some of the key characteristics of most of the famous MG cars are their smallness, their affordability and low running costs, their performance (modest in absolute terms yet typically outstanding for their size), their safe handling and good-natured, untemperamental behaviour, and also their design. Not only were MGs good-looking, pretty little cars, but with the J2 Midget of 1932 the marque set the standard for a generation of British sports cars. In 1951 the Museum of Modern Art in New York held an exhibition entitled '8 automobiles', a display of eight cars which 'were chosen primarily for their excellence as works of art'. Is it any surprise that one of the eight was an MG Midget, the TC model? Quoting from the exhibition catalogue, its 'stylistic understatement is the result of an intense but devious preoccupation with

'Old Number One', the first proper MG sports car, was built for Cecil Kimber to drive in the Land's End Trial in March 1925.

Before the arrival of the Midget, MG's staple product was the Morris- **based sporting tourer, typified by this 1926 14/28 Bullnose model.**

This M-type, purchased by Edsel Ford in 1930, is believed to have been **the first MG in the USA, and is now in a car museum in Pennsylvania.**

appearance'. Only slightly less extravagant praise came from George Oliver, who in *A History of Coachbuilding* (1962) stated, 'The MG Midget was one of those inspired designs that shows no signs even now, more than twenty-five years after its introduction, of dating in any significant way. Until recently there have been hardly any bad-looking MG cars. Perhaps the late Cecil Kimber was solely responsible for this consistently high standard: I do not know for certain – but the fact remains that it was maintained for the best part of twenty years'.

The story of MG starts with two men, two very different personalities who despite their dissimilar aims became united in the MG venture. William Morris, later Lord Nuffield (1877-1963), was the legendary motor tycoon who started out at the age of 16 as a cycle mechanic with a working capital of 5 shillings. Within 25 years he built Britain's biggest motor business, earning himself a fortune which was distributed for charitable purposes, largely within his lifetime. Yet despite his success Morris in later years found himself increasingly out of tune with the ever more complicated business of running his company. Some of his actions almost destroyed Morris Motors Limited, but he clung to power until at the age of 75 he finally surrendered control by letting his company merge with Austin. The name and reputation of Morris as a make of car were founded on and upheld by the company's ability to provide the British motorist with a quality product in the popular car market: cars like the original Bullnose Morris of the 1920s, the Morris Eight of the 1930s or the post-war Morris Minor, all of them affordable to buy and run, and above all easy for even a novice to operate, as well as

being rewarding for the more discerning motorist.

Cecil Kimber (1888-1945) was small of stature, with a slight limp which was the legacy of a motorcycle accident in his youth. From an early age he was a keen motorcyclist, soon a motorist of sporting inclination. He left his father's printing business to start a career in the motor industry, working for several different companies before joining Morris Garages as sales manager in 1921. By this time he had built up a lot of useful experience in works organisation, buying and engineering. Morris Garages at Oxford, William Morris's original business, was now a distributor and dealer for Morris cars and was still in Morris's personal control. In 1921 the Bullnose Morris car had barely set out on its remarkable career – that year's output from the Cowley factory was hardly more than 3000 cars – but Morris had begun his famous series of price cuts. By 1925 over 1000 were leaving the factory almost every week.

It was Kimber's good fortune to join Morris at exactly the point in time when its success was about to take off. In 1922 he was promoted to general manager of Morris Garages. While demand for the standard Morris Cowley and Oxford models never slackened, Kimber perceived that there was a demand, however small, for different versions of the basic product. He arranged for Morris chassis to be delivered to Morris Garages, there to be fitted with special bodies which often were the result of his own ideas on car design. Kimber turned out to be a competent body designer and his preoccupation with the way a car looked was instrumental in making his cars so successful. The classic MG radiator was one of his inspirations, as was the octagonal badge.

Cecil Kimber in his bay-windowed office at Abingdon. On his desk are a model of the Magic Midget and the tiger mascot for the 'Tigresse' Mark III (or 18/100) racing model of 1930.

Early efforts at making special-bodied Morris cars were quite modest. The first design was a 'chummy' version of the Morris Cowley, a close-coupled open four-seater which was soon supplanted when a similar body style appeared in the standard range. Kimber then ordered a series of two-seater bodies from Raworth, and the first sale of a Morris Cowley fitted with such a body took place in August 1923. In early 1924 he also produced a luxurious four-door saloon on the Morris Oxford chassis, and began to advertise the two-seater as the 'MG Super Sports Morris'. By this time the first definitive MG had appeared. It was a handsome four-seater with a body supplied by Carbodies fitted on the 14/28 Morris Oxford chassis, the first car of this type being delivered in March 1924.

Many years later Kimber was to express his philosophy 'that if a firm could offer the public a product only ten per cent better than anyone else's, that firm could command a fifty per cent better price'. In 1924 the MG Super Sports four-seater cost £395, while the cheapest Morris Oxford four-seater came down to £275 in September. Was the MG version then ten per cent better? It was certainly much more attractive, with its low build, raked windscreen, wheel discs and bodywork partly finished in polished aluminium. The MG was a sporting tourer, not quite a sports car – yet. The first proper MG sports car was a one-off built for Kimber himself to drive in the 1925 Land's End Trial. It had an unusual overhead-valve version of the sidevalve Hotchkiss engine found in Morris cars, and used a

modified Cowley chassis with semi-elliptic rear springs, together with the Oxford's bigger four-wheel brakes. The car was ready just in time for the trial in March 1925 – and has since entered history under the name of 'Old Number One'.

With a variety of body styles, the Bullnose MG 14/28 models sold increasingly well during 1925. It became difficult to extend production in the cramped premises in Alfred Lane, one of Morris Garages' several locations, so in September 1925 MG production was moved to the new Morris Radiators factory in Bainton Road on the outskirts of Oxford. A year later, the Bullnose Morris Cowley and Oxford models were replaced by the new Flatnose versions, and in due course MG followed suit, bringing out the Flatnose 14/28, which after only a few months gave way to a further improved model, the 14/40 or Mark IV type. By then MG was once again looking for new premises as Morris Radiators wanted their factory back due to expanding production. Cecil Kimber went to William Morris, who sanctioned the construction of a new MG factory in Edmund Road, Cowley, to which MG moved in September 1927. Despite the upheavals of the move, production in 1927 topped 400 cars, almost double the 1926 figure.

Kimber realised that in addition to the new factory he would need new products to replace the ageing sidevalve design, and proceeded to fashion two additional strings to his bow. One was in effect a six-cylinder development of the existing MG theme, a luxurious fast sporting tourer using a new 2½-litre overhead camshaft engine developed by Morris Engines for a new Morris car (the Light Six/Six which was later replaced by the Isis). This was fitted into MG's first specially designed chassis and the result was the MG 18/80, which was introduced at the 1928 Motor Show and which in various forms continued in production until 1933. Offered with a variety of bodies from luxury saloons to the stark racing-inspired Speed Model, the 18/80 was quite successful in its class but was comparatively expensive at £500 to £700, so production was always on a modest scale.

Meanwhile, William Morris had bought the bankrupt Wolseley company of Birmingham. Since 1919 Wolseley had made a range of small cars with overhead camshaft engines based on the design of a Hispano-Suiza aero engine which it had built under licence during World War One. The Wolseley Ten and the later 11/22 models were well made but always too expensive to compete in the popular market, and except for a few specially built racers they were quite without sporting pretensions. Wolseley's financial affairs deteriorated to the point where a receiver was called in, and in early 1927 William Morris bought the company.

He gave the Wolseley designers a brief to develop a small 8hp car to bring Morris into competition with the well-established Austin Seven. The resulting car featured an 847cc engine with an overhead camshaft in the Wolseley tradition driven by a vertical shaft at the front of the engine, the same shaft acting as the armature shaft for the dynamo. Unlike the Austin Seven, the new small Morris had proper coupled four-wheel brakes and semi-elliptic springs front and rear. The car was launched in August 1928 and bore the name Morris Minor. Available as a two-door fabric saloon for £135 or in open tourer form for £10 less, it had about 20bhp on tap and was able to out-perform the Austin Seven, but it was never quite the rival to the Seven that Morris had hoped.

Cecil Kimber was quick to realise the possibilities inherent in the advanced engine design of the new small Morris, and his second new model of 1928 was a small sports car based on the Minor, with a standard Minor engine in a barely modified chassis fitted with an open two-seater body. To introduce so small a sports car was an unusual step, if not quite unprecedented, for there had been sporting and racing versions of the Austin Seven from 1923 onwards. By 1928 the most important ones were the Gordon England Cup model which cost only £150 and of which more than 900 were made in 1928 alone, the new Swallow two-seater which cost £175 and of which probably some 500 were made during the first year, and Austin's own Super Sports model, fitted with a supercharger and effectively a works racing model although it was listed at £225. Another small sports car was Triumph's new Super Seven, available in two-seater 'de luxe' form for £167 10s, but with a top speed of around 50mph its performance was not much better than the Austin Seven's. The supercharged Special Sports model of 1929 was a good deal faster but cost £250. The only other important manufacturer of 8hp cars was Singer whose Junior, like the Morris Minor, had an overhead camshaft engine of 847cc although only developing 16.5bhp in standard form. The Porlock sports version made little impression; Singer's best small sports cars were yet to come.

Rumours that MG was planning an unusual new model began to appear in the press soon after the launch of the Morris Minor, *The Autocar* in September 1928 announcing that MG would launch a sports model of the Minor which it then referred to as the *Morris* Midget. The magazine made handsome amends when the car was officially introduced in the following month, declaring

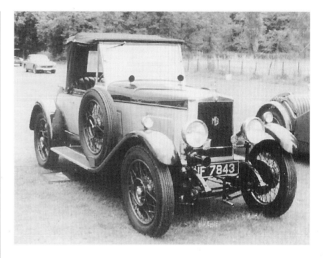

By late 1927, MG had progressed to the Flatnose model which superseded Morris's Bullnose family, this 14/40 two-seater looking a little ungainly with the hood erected.

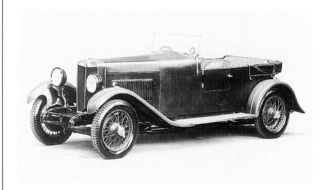

Appearing at the same time as the M-type was the MG 18/80 Mark I model, this one the Speed Model which appeared in 1930.

'The MG Midget will make sports car history'. Also at the time known as the 8/33hp model – the '8' indicating RAC or tax horsepower, the '33' being a rather optimistic estimate of bhp – this first Midget was a pretty little boat-tailed two-seater, priced to match the Austin Swallow at £175 but with much better performance than its rival: no Austin Seven based car with a sidevalve engine in standard form without a supercharger could match the 65mph which was well within the capabilities of the new MG. Indeed, the Midget was almost a match for the MG 14/40 in terms of performance, despite having an engine of half the size. It was a classic case of 'small is beautiful', and small the car was: its interior was distinctly cramped for anybody who was only slightly bigger than Kimber!

MIDGET CHRONICLE

From the introduction of the M-type at the 1928 London Motor Show until the November day in 1979 when the last MG Midget 1500 was manufactured, Midget history spans 51 years – and as this also all but represents the period during which MGs were made at Abingdon, Midget history is inextricably linked with the history of The MG Car Company Limited. The company in fact preceded the first Midget by a matter of a few months only; it was in the spring of 1928 that The MG Car Company (Proprietors: Morris Garages Ltd) was first officially established, with the company name beginning to appear on chassis number plates and in literature, and the 1928 Motor Show stand on which the M-type made its debut was MG's first Motor Show display in its own right.

In September 1927 MG production had moved into the new, purpose-built factory in Edmund Road, Cowley, and it was here that production of the M-type got under way in March 1929. A delay of almost six months from introduction until the first cars could be delivered to customers was then still acceptable, especially

The later M-types with metal-panelled bodies could be spotted by the squared-off wing section with a central ridge (facing page). Two tread strips on the running board indicate that this is a TC (top). The wings of the final J2s, built from 1933, were swept instead of cycle-type (above). This brochure rendering appears to show midgets in a Midget!

as the peak season for new car sales in the pre-war years was the period from Easter to Whitsun. In those days many new models launched with a flourish at the autumn motor show were little more than prototypes, going into production only if enough orders were received. There was never such a question mark over the future of the M-type, with eager customers snapping up the cars as soon as they began to emerge in quantity.

The success of the new model was the main reason why MG soon outgrew the Edmund Road factory. A search for bigger premises was instigated and was crowned with success when a disused factory was found in Abingdon, some miles south of Oxford, then just across the Berkshire border, in a picturesque location on the Thames. The factory was owned by the Pavlova Leather Company and had been built during World War One but had since fallen into disuse, Pavlova's operations being concentrated in a smaller factory next door. Agreement was reached for MG to lease Pavlova works (the company only bought the factory in 1939). By the end of September 1929, the move from Edmund Road had been completed and increasing numbers of M-types were coming off the new assembly lines.

The other important step was that The MG Car Company Limited was set up in its own right on 21 July 1930. The issued share capital was 19,000 £1 shares of which 18,995 were bought by Morris Industries Limited – William Morris's personal holding company – and five were held, respectively, by William Morris himself, by Cecil Kimber, and by Morris's secretary, solicitor and accountant. Cecil Kimber was appointed managing director and William Morris took the title of governing director. A few days later MG bought from Morris Garages Ltd 'all assets connected with the business of The MG Car Company' as from 31 December 1929 for the sum of £18,995, and in October 1930 the lease on Pavlova works was formally assigned by Morris Garages to The MG Car Company Limited. To give the new company working capital, loans totalling £30,000 were advanced by Morris Industries Limited. Although Morris Garages had been paid only £18,995 for the MG business, the first annual accounts of The MG Car Company Limited reveal that the company's stock of cars, parts and work in progress as at 1 January 1930 had been valued at £74,620, while at the end of 1930 the assets on the balance sheet were £115,518.

Now well established in what would remain its home for 50 years, MG soon extended its activities. 1931 saw a cluster of new models, starting with the C-type or Montlhéry Midget, the first catalogued racing version,

followed by the long-wheelbase D-type with a four-seater body. There was also the F-type Magna, first of MG's small sixes, with a Wolseley Hornet derived engine of 1271cc. In 1932 the J-types appeared, the J1 four-seater and J2 two-seater replacing the D-type and M-type respectively, while the J3 and J4 were supercharged racing models. There was also the K-type Magnette, another six-cylinder model but with engine capacity reduced to 1087cc to bring it into the international 1100cc class for racing. A new Magna, the L-type with the 1087cc engine, followed in 1933, and 1934 saw two important new models: the P-type (PA) Midget, and the N-type (NA) Magnette, the latter with the 1271cc engine size (sometimes quoted as 1287cc). Also in 1934 came the Q-type racing Midget, soon replaced by the R-type, last of the racing Midgets, which made its debut in early 1935.

This was a watershed year in MG history. Leonard Lord was appointed managing director of MG as he already was of Morris, with Cecil Kimber taking the title of general manager (he was reinstated as managing director at the end of 1936 after Lord had left Morris), and the Morris Industries Ltd shareholding was sold to Morris Motors Ltd. MG announced that it was to stop making racing cars, and pulled out of competition activities. At the 1935 Motor Show a new MG model was introduced – the SA Two-litre model, a luxurious sports saloon the like of which MG had not made since the 18/80 Mark II had been discontinued in 1933. It incorporated a higher proportion of standard

The year is 1929 BA – Before Abingdon. This was how M-type assembly progressed in the factory in Edmund Road, Cowley (right). Aerial view of the Abingdon factory in 1933 (facing page). Ironically enough, these original buildings, with the administration block at far right, survive today – most of the post-war expansions have been demolished.

Morris/Wolseley components than had been MG's practice for some time, including an engine whose overhead valves were operated by pushrods and rockers rather than directly from an overhead camshaft.

The line of overhead camshaft MGs came to an end in 1936, when the P-type Midget was replaced by the TA, and the N-type Magnette by the VA 1½-litre range. In 1938 the model range was extended by the WA, a 2.6-litre derivative of the SA. Although the new cars were viewed with scorn by many an MG *aficionado,* they sold very well indeed, and MG set a new production record with almost 3000 cars made in 1937 alone. The last new model introduced before the war was the short-lived 1939 TB, just like the TA but fitted with a new and rather better engine. Behind the scenes a new saloon design was reaching the prototype stage, the so-called MG 'Ten', which used the TB engine and had a body based on the contemporary Morris Eight.

War interrupted these developments, however, and the Abingdon factory was quickly reorganised for wartime production, turning out most famously the front section of the Albemarle aircraft, but also making a variety of light tanks. Sadly, during the war MG lost its founder and managing director: Kimber was dismissed from the Nuffield Organisation in 1941 for having failed to fit in with the company's overall strategy for war production. He was killed in a railway accident in 1945. After Kimber's departure H. A. Ryder was appointed MG's managing director; he came from Morris Radiators, which he had helped to set up in 1919, and

left little impression on MG (although he is said to have disapproved of sporting activities), resigning from Morris Motors in 1947 in a boardroom purge. The man in everyday charge at Abingdon was long-serving general manager George Propert, replaced in 1949 by Jack Tatlow, an ex-Riley man who came down from Coventry when Riley production moved to Abingdon.

It was Propert who got MG back into car production in 1945 with the TC model – a modified TB – followed in 1947 by the YA saloon, the production version of the 1940 MG Ten prototype. While there was a multitude of Morris-inspired plans for future MG production, the only project which came to fruition was the updated and much modernised TD Midget of 1950, in turn followed by the facelifted TF model of 1953. By then, Morris Motors had merged with Austin to form BMC, while in the same year of 1952 Tatlow was succeeded as general manager by John Thornley, the accountant and founder member of the MG Car Club who had served the company since 1930.

Thornley's overriding priority was to get a new sports car into production, and MG's chief engineer Syd Enever had designed an all-new streamlined car which was to be fitted with BMC's 1.5-litre B-series engine, also found in the ZA Magnette saloon introduced in 1953. The new sports car was for a time held up by Sir Leonard Lord, now managing director of BMC, but was finally cleared for production and was introduced in September 1955 as the MGA. The car might have been the UA-series but it was decided to call it the MGA to signify that the new

model marked a new beginning for MG, and with it MG for a time left the original Midget concept behind.

It was six years before a new MG Midget appeared. In the meantime, Abingdon had become the home of not only MG but also Austin-Healey, production of the 100-Six model being moved down from Longbridge in 1957. In 1958, the big Healey was supplemented by the Healey-designed Sprite model, a small low-cost sports car based on standard BMC small car components including the famous A-series engine. It quickly established itself as the most successful small sports car on the market, with over 50,000 being made in three years. In 1961 an improved Sprite Mark II was introduced, followed within a few weeks by an MG version which brought back the Midget name. At 948cc this was the smallest MG since the demise of the PB in 1936.

The badge-engineered 'Spridget' twins were very successful, the Midget being a sort of 'de-luxe' version selling at a slightly higher price, but the 1960s saw increasing competition in the sports car market, especially for sales in the all-important USA, and in 1962 Triumph's first Spitfire became the main rival for the Spridgets. It also spurred on BMC to make worthwhile improvements to their small sports car which, among other changes, acquired bigger engines: 1098cc in 1962

To underline the TD's appeal in an international (or at least American) market, this brochure illustration showed it cruising along the Grand Canyon (above). Not universally admired when new, the attractive lines of the TF (facing page) have since ensured it a large following.

and 1275cc in 1966. With changes in American legislation special versions had to be developed for this market in 1967. Then, in 1968, BMC merged with Leyland, which already owned Triumph, bringing the two rivals into the same fold. The new British Leyland company's chairman was Donald Stokes, who in 1970 cancelled the agreement to use the Healey name, and the Sprite model was discontinued shortly afterwards, leaving the MG Midget on its own. In 1974 it became the Midget 1500, using the engine from the Triumph Spitfire, and in this form it continued in production until November 1979.

By then British Leyland had been effectively nationalised after running into financial problems, and Michael Edwardes had been appointed chief executive in 1977, with a free hand to sort out the troubles of the ailing company. His first plan for large-scale cutbacks was announced in September 1979, and part of the agenda was the closure of MG's Abingdon factory, with both the

Midget and the MGB going out of production. The last car, a Limited Edition MGB GT, was built at Abingdon in October 1980, after which the factory was closed down and sold.

The MG name was not in abeyance for long, as in 1982 the MG Metro was introduced as a sporting version of the popular new Austin small car. It was followed by similar MG Maestro and Montego models which remained in production throughout the 1980s. In 1986 the parent company BL was renamed Rover Group, and in 1988 the much slimmed-down company was sold to British Aerospace. Plans were already under way then to reintroduce an MG sports car, with many different rumours appearing in the press from time to time. As a rather cautious first step, it was decided to bring back a developed MGB, a move made possible by the activities of British Motor Heritage – a Rover subsidiary which in 1988 had brought the MGB Roadster bodyshell back into production for the purpose of re-shelling old MGBs. In 1992 the MG RV8 was introduced, featuring a restyled Heritage-built MGB bodyshell and the 3.9-litre V8 engine from the Range Rover. This was obviously no Midget, but even at a price of £25,000 Rover had little trouble selling the planned production run of 2000 cars, many being exported to Japan. In 1994 MG came

under new ownership yet again when Rover Group was bought by the respected German car manufacturer BMW, a company with an equally strong sporting heritage and a great belief in tradition.

The stage was now cleared for the introduction of the long-awaited all-new MG sports car in 1995. A small, reasonably priced open two-seater, the MGF was truly a return to the original MG and MG Midget values, and it also followed MG traditions by making extensive use of standard mass-produced Rover parts including the twin-cam 16-valve all-aluminium K-series engine – but in other respects it was a complete break with traditional MG sports car design, being the first mid-engined production model to bear the brown and cream octagonal badge. With a target production figure of 25,000 cars per year from the Rover factory at Longbridge in Birmingham – the original Austin factory founded 90 years before – the new MG was clearly going to be a serious contender in the international sports car market, which for quite some time had been dominated by Japanese manufacturers. What better omen could there be for the new MG than that its launch all but coincided with the 70th anniversary of 'Old Number One', the car that Cecil Kimber himself always considered to be the first real MG?

OVERHEAD CAMSHAFT MIDGETS

The Berkshire-issued RX registration suggests this is a company-owned M-type, here on the test hill at Brooklands, the occasion unknown.

Here driven by L.A.Welch in the 1930 London to Land's End Trial, WL 7180 was at the time the company's demonstrator M-type and was also road tested by both *The Motor* and *The Light Car*. It was a very early 1929 car, and had raced at Brooklands in the JCC High-Speed Trial in June 1929.

To return to 1929: the new MG Midget which went on sale in March was, as far as chassis and engine were concerned, only slightly modified from its Morris Minor parent. The channel-section frame with its simple crossmembers was not changed at all but the suspension was slightly lowered and the steering column was raked further back. The 8in drum brakes were rod operated, with the rods for the front brakes mounted on the outside of the car, and the handbrake worked on the transmission. The engine was in the same state of tune as in the Morris Minor and with its minuscule 1⅛in SU side-draught carburettor developed 20bhp at 4000rpm – an adequate figure from 847cc at the time. The overhead camshaft was driven by a vertical shaft set at the front of the engine and passing through the Lucas dynamo, and the slightly inclined, staggered valves were activated through adjustable rocker arms. The crankshaft had only two main bearings but was short enough to be sufficiently rigid. Both inlet and exhaust manifolds were on the left-hand side of the engine, the exhaust manifold

The M-type's Morris Minor ancestry was well camouflaged. This 1930 model is an Abingdon-built car, with cable-operated brakes and doors hinged at the front.

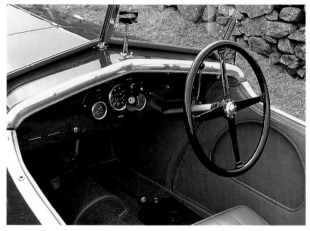

This restored M-type interior is finished to a rather higher standard that originally by MG. The Rotax instrument and switch panel in black with black dials, and the higher-placed speedometer, indicates that this is one of the later cars, in fact a 1932 metal-panelled model.

Under the bonnet of an M-type. Apart from a few octagons, such as on the camshaft cover, the engine was at first unmodified Morris Minor. The vertically-mounted dynamo at the front was frequently troublesome because of oil leaks from the cylinder head.

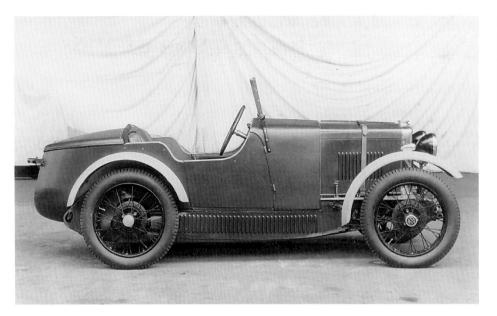

This was one of the original works M-types built for the 1930 Double-Twelve race at Brooklands, and later followed by a series of '12/12 Replicas'.

being heavily ribbed and featuring a prominent octagonal MG badge. There was a single dry-plate clutch, and the gearbox had three forward speeds, the gear lever being cranked more sharply back than on the Minor. The gear ratios were the same as on the Minor.

The radiator was a miniature version of the one introduced on the six-cylinder 18/80 model, and marque identity was further stressed by the MG badges on the tiny hubcaps; otherwise the bolt-on wire wheels with three-stud mounting were those of the Morris Minor. The boat-tailed two-seater body, constructed largely from plywood covered in blue or red fabric, was supplied by Carbodies in Coventry; MG's initial order was for 500 bodies at £6 10s each. On the early cars the doors were hinged at the rear. Skimpy cycle type wings were fitted but the front wings did not turn with the wheels, being fixed to the chassis and braced to each other. The bonnet was painted body colour, the wings and wheels typically black. The cover of the tail lifted up to reveal the spare wheel and sufficient room to stow the hood if not much else. The petrol tank was mounted on the scuttle. The windscreen was of a rakish swept-back V shape with a simple half frame. The hood was very simple, weather protection being generally inadequate as no sidescreens were provided.

The cockpit could best be described as snug, with a single bench seat for driver and passenger. Instead of the three-spoke steering wheel of the Minor, a more sporty four-spoke wheel was provided, but on the other hand the centrally-mounted oval instrument panel was undiluted Morris. Made of polished brass, it contained an

ammeter, a speedometer and an oil pressure gauge, all with white faces, the central speedometer being set at a lower level than the two flanking smaller instruments. The Lucas (or Rotax) lighting set comprised two headlamps, two wing-mounted sidelamps and a single tail lamp. There was nothing superfluous or remotely luxurious in the way of equipment, not even a windscreen wiper.

When the M-type was tested by the leading

RX 6795 was the M-type which made 100 consecutive ascents of the Beggar's Roost hill in 1930. The bracket on the tail is for a second spare wheel, fitted to the car when it ran in the London-Edinburgh trial.

The four-seater D-type of 1931 was the first Midget for the family man – at the cost of much of the M-type's performance.

magazines in the summer of 1929 it drew much praise for its performance, with a top speed of 65mph and a modest thirst for petrol of 38-40mpg. *The Motor* found that 'the MG Midget fills a real niche in the sports car world … it is one of the most fascinating little vehicles we have ever driven', echoing *The Autocar* which summed up the Midget as 'an extraordinarily fascinating little car, both to look at and to handle on the road'. In the autumn the Midget was improved in a number of respects: most of these modifications took place at around the time production was moved from Cowley to Abingdon, thus offering a useful way of distinguishing cars from the two factories. The brake system was thoroughly revised, operation now being by cable and the handbrake functioning on all four wheels. The doors became hinged at the front, and the instrument panel was slightly changed so that the speedometer was positioned above the smaller dials, while instrument faces became black. The price was increased to £185. An additional body style was introduced at the 1929 Motor Show, the charming little Sportsman's Coupé, again with a fabric body. It had a sliding sunroof with four glass panels, the interior was nicely furnished with full leather and carpet trim, there were individual bucket seats and even a totally useless rear seat. It cost £245 – rather expensive compared with the £187 10s charged for an Austin Seven Swallow saloon. Still, quite a few M-type coupés were made over the next couple of years.

The M-type's competition career, more fully recounted in the next chapter, began as early as 1929, but a special competition model was only evolved in 1930,

being named the Double-Twelve Replica – or '12/12' – after the Brooklands race where it made its debut. On these race cars the engine was mildly tuned, a different camshaft giving some overlap in the valve timing to raise power output to 27bhp. From late 1930 this camshaft was incorporated on all production cars and at the same time a four-speed gearbox was made available as an optional extra for a rather steep £20 – even more expensive was a supercharger installation at £65. The accelerator pedal was moved from the centre to the right side and a more convenient double-cranked gear lever was fitted.

Production of the M-type continued into 1932, that year's models having metal-panelled instead of fabric bodies – this applied to the two-seater as well as the coupé – and these later cars also had wings of angular cross section, while the horn was mounted externally in the valance panel between the front dumb-irons. For a while the fabric-bodied two-seater was still listed at the reduced price of £165, while the metal-panelled version cost £185 and the coupé was reduced to £235. With the metal-panelled bodies a wider choice of colour schemes became available, including two-tone combinations.

Quite a few M-types had been sold in chassis form and fitted with a variety of special bodies; one of the better-known was the Jarvis, a two-seater with a flat back and externally mounted spare wheel. Its shape hinted at MG's next two-seater, the J2. The London distributor University Motors offered a coupé-based drophead model which they called a 'Foursome'. MG themselves built a one-off M-type based van, known as the MG High Speed Service Van – 'high speed' probably being relative. This was an unusual but charming advertising vehicle, and while the original is long gone, a replica has been lovingly constructed by a latter day enthusiast.

The Morris Minor chassis obviously had its limitations for future sports car development. Probably in 1930 MG acquired an example of the little-known French Rally sports car, which had several features that MG's chief engineer, Hubert N. Charles, was to incorporate in succeeding Midgets. These included the chassis design, of very low build, with parallel side members which continued straight under the rear axle and swept up over the front axle, to which Charles added tubular crossmembers, while the rear ends of the springs were mounted in sliding bronze trunnions. The first tangible result was the first Midget record car, the EX120, soon followed by the C-type or Montlhéry Midget, a catalogued racing model; both are described in the following chapter. Then came the D-type, introduced at the 1931 Motor Show together with MG's first small six, the F-type Magna. The D-type was a long-wheelbase model, at first with 7ft between the axles, later extended

to 7ft 2in, compared to the 6ft 6in of the M-type. The new chassis design was used on the D-type, which was offered only with four-seater coachwork, either in open form or as a closed 'Salonette'. The engine was the same 27bhp unit as found on later M-types, and a three-speed gearbox was still standard, although now fitted with a remote control gearchange. Another change from the M-type was that the D-type had centre-lock Rudge Whitworth type wheels, with twin-eared knock-ons. The petrol tank was mounted at the rear, and an SU 'Petrolift' fuel pump was used.

At £210 the D-type had some appeal to the Midget enthusiast with a growing family but it was heavy and not as quick as the M-type. Another drawback was that if the passenger carrying capacity was used to the full, handling was adversely affected – not surprising as the rear seat passengers' weight was well behind the rear axle. The D-type remained in production for less than a year and was not particularly popular. The Salonette was always a rare vehicle and it seems that no survivors with this type of body are known.

This delightful rendering of an M-type Sportsman's Coupé is by Connolly, who for many years was MG's most prolific brochure artist.

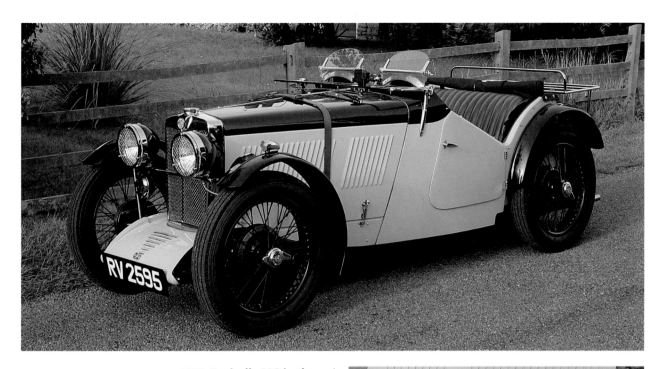

Sports car of the year, 1932 style. The J2 was a genuine sensation, offering unrivalled performance for its size and price. The model set the pattern for the styling of all later Midgets, right through to 1955. Typically MG in the liberal use of octagons for the instrument bezels, the J2 dashboard had an engine-turned finish. Additional scales on the rev counter showed speeds in third and top gears.

On the J-type engine with the cross-flow cylinder head, the carburettors moved to the ignition side. The large plate on the cam cover gave detailed instructions for engine adjustments. Chassis lubrication featured grouped grease nipples, in the lower corner by the firewall.

The J1 was in terms of performance a great improvement over the D-type but had an almost identical body with the exception of the line at the top of the door and body side.

In August 1932 the M-, C- and D-types were all swept away and a new, much improved and rationalised Midget range was introduced: the J-types, initially available as the J1 four-seater and J2 two-seater, soon followed by the supercharged J3 and J4 racing models. All the new cars had what was basically the D-type chassis, with a common wheelbase of 7ft 2in regardless of body style. The engine was substantially improved, with the cross-flow 'AB' type cylinder head first pioneered on later C-types, and individual inlet and exhaust ports for

This J2 was the original road test car which in the hands of *The Autocar* **reached 80mph, after the engine had been prepared at Abingdon.**

all cylinders. The inlet manifold moved to the right-hand side of the cylinder head, and two SU carburettors were fitted. Power output was usefully increased to 36bhp at 5500rpm – something which the crankshaft, still of the two-bearing type, found difficulty in coping with! Most striking was the new two-seater body. With the J2

Classic cutaway drawing by Max Millar, one of the best exponents of this technique, shows the simplicity and neatness of the J2 design.

Kimber had hit upon the timeless formula for sports car design: the flared scuttle with twin humps and a fold-flat windscreen, the deep elbow cut-outs in the doors, the flat back with a slab-type petrol tank and an external spare wheel carrier, as well as all the right trimmings for a sports car, including a combined rev counter and speedometer in front of the driver, an engine-turned finish to the dashboard, a quick-action filler cap, and the oft-seen extra fittings of stoneguards for the headlamps and a leather strap across the bonnet.

All this was available for just £199 10s, with the equally pretty if not quite so rakish J1 four-seater at £220 and the same car in Salonette form at £255. The J-types had performance to match their looks. Admittedly the road test car submitted to *The Autocar* had been specially tuned to reach the 80mph top speed recorded by the magazine – in consequence it broke its crankshaft within a few days – but almost any J2 would reach an easy 75mph, the four-seaters being slightly slower. The J3, basically a supercharged J2 although fitted with the 746cc engine, became available by the end of 1932, and the proper racing J4 followed in the spring of 1933. Both were appreciably faster than the J2 but were correspondingly more costly – the J4 cost £495, well over double the price of a J2.

MG was by now well established as the leading manufacturer of small sports cars, with an enviable list of competition successes. Of the rest, Austin had discontinued the limited production Ulster sports version of the Seven (offered during 1930-31 at £185 in standard 65mph form or £225 for the supercharged model) and the new '65' (or 'Nippy') sports model of June 1933 was no match for the performance of the J2: with 23bhp the Nippy was flat out at 55mph, although at around £150

its price was attractive. At the other end of the spectrum was the admirable but very expensive Riley Nine Brooklands. In 1934 Riley brought out another Nine-based sports model, the Imp, which at around £300 was well outside the MG market. The strongest rival for MG was now Singer, the 972cc overhead camshaft Nine being developed into the Le Mans model of 1934. This cost £215 in two-seater form but, of the bewildering range of Singer Nine sporting models, it was the 75mph Le Mans Special Speed model, magneto ignition and all, which in terms of performance was the nearest MG rival, at £225. These Singers were deservedly popular, some 2000 being sold in 1934 alone, and had a following on the continent, competing in large numbers against the MGs at for instance Le Mans, but proper Singer sports cars disappeared for good after 1936.

For 1934 the J2 was slightly revised with swept instead of cycle type wings, although by the 1933 Motor Show the J1 four-seaters had been discontinued, as had the J3 and J4 racing models. The swept-wing J2 was not as pleasing in appearance as the original model – the wings looked rather like the afterthought they were – but with wings on all three MG models (K-type Magnette, L-type Magna and J2) now being of this quite distinctive design, it was a valuable marque recognition point. The later J2s had slight changes to the engine as well, including a raised compression ratio and pistons with controlled-expansion skirts and fully-floating gudgeon pins. In its final form the J2 stayed in production for only about six months, being replaced in March 1934 by the

The J1 four-seater did not make such a radical statement of style as the J2. In fact the car was very similar to the D-type, with the same **wings and the flat scuttle – from the exterior only the deep elbow cut-outs in the top of the doors indicated that this was a new model.**

third generation MG Midget, the thoroughly improved P-type – or PA-type in its original form.

By now it seemed that MG had learned their lesson. The most fundamental improvement on the PA was the new crankshaft with three main bearings, banishing for good the J-type's unhealthy appetite for crankshafts. The cylinder block was redesigned and the cylinder head design further improved, with a larger diameter camshaft. The vertical dynamo drive arrangement for the overhead camshaft was retained. The engine, still made by Wolseley, was now rather more special than originally intended, and was produced exclusively for MG to its specification: the overhead camshaft Morris Minor had been discontinued in 1932, and although there was now a small 9hp Wolseley car, this used a 60×90mm 1018cc engine of rather different specification, with chain drive

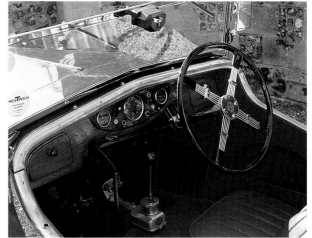

The J2 dashboard was very much like the D-type's, with a simple speedometer for the central instrument panel. There was no proper oil pressure gauge, only a strange Jaeger 'oil **pressure indicator' with four slits in a propeller shape in the dial, through which a red background could be seen if the pressure dropped below the safe limit.**

A rather flattering Connolly rendering of the J1 Salonette, which was in fact a boxy little car.

One of the best-looking MGs. The Airline coupé was available on both the PA and PB chassis, while small numbers of N-type Magnettes and two TAs also had this body. This car is a PA.

The J3 was, broadly speaking, a J2 fitted with the supercharged 746cc engine instead of the normally-aspirated 847cc engine.

The J4 was a pure racing model, fitted with a larger supercharger than the J3, a special doorless body, larger brake drums and a Brooklands-regulation silencer and fish-tail for the exhaust.

for the overhead camshaft. The power output of the PA engine was quoted as 34.9bhp at 5000rpm, and an immediate recognition point of the new engine was the octagonal quick-release oil filler cap on top of the valve cover. A water pump was also now available as an optional extra.

The chassis was improved in detail, the wheelbase being slightly lengthened to the unhandy dimension of 7ft 3⁵⁄₁₆in. First and second gear ratios were slightly lower, to improve the Midget's low-gear acceleration and make it more suitable as a trials car. The biggest change to the chassis specification was the 12in brake drums now fitted, the same size as on the Magna and Magnette, though they were still mechanically operated, by cables. Two-

The P-type – or PA – of 1934 had a substantially improved engine with a three-bearing crankshaft. This model had the swept wings from the start.

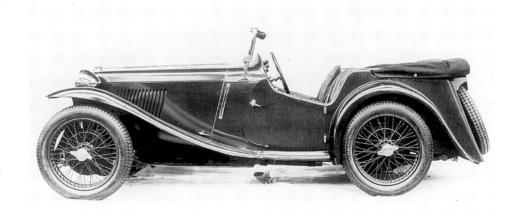

As might be judged from the proportions of this side view, in four-seater form the P-type was a little tail-heavy when used to capacity.

and four-seater open bodies were available on the new chassis, of similar design back to the doors, and with swept wings rather better integrated in the design than had been the case with the final J2. The P-type had built-in trafficators, on either side of the scuttle. The dashboard was finished in wood veneer and had an improved layout, with a central switch panel also incorporating the mileometer, the combined rev counter/speedometer still in front of the driver, and the smaller instruments and lighting/ignition switch in a matching octagonal surround in front of the passenger.

The two-seater was increased in price to £222, and the four-seater cost £240. In addition there was a new closed body – not the boxy salonette as seen on the J1

On the P-types (this two-seater is a PA), the swept wings were fully integrated in the main design. These were the only Midgets to have built-in trafficators on either side of the scuttle.

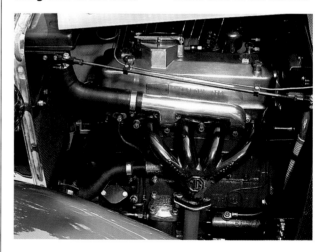

The PA's veneered dashboard, with a central combined switch panel and mileometer. Octagonal knobs were used for gear lever and engine controls. Dashboard plaque is from University Motors Ltd, the MG distributor.

PA engine with a splendid four-branch exhaust manifold and the bright water inlet manifold above. Octagons can be seen just about everywhere, including the large quick-release oil filler cap and the exhaust manifold.

Later PB models featured a slatted radiator – the first on a Midget. This was the last Midget to be offered with four-seater coachwork. Even those sidelamps are now octagonal...

chassis but a two-seater 'Airline' coupé with a streamlined swept tail, offering reasonable luggage accommodation behind the two bucket seats. This was not cheap at £290 but was a comfortable and well-appointed little car, with the characteristic MG feature of a sliding sunroof with inset glass panels. It was quite the prettiest body style in the range, without a doubt one of the best-looking MG cars ever made, and because of the streamlined coachwork it was also expected to be faster than the open P-types, even though it was somewhat heavier. It was never road-tested, and when PA two-seaters were put through their paces by the magazines, *The Motor* and *The Light Car* agreed that the top speed was 76mph while *The Autocar* managed only 74mph. These figures may have been a disappointment after that original J2 road test but in the case of the P-type there is little doubt that the measured top speeds more accurately reflected the performance of actual production cars.

By 1934 the racing Midgets were being developed on

The PB dashboard for the first time had a separate speedometer as well as a rev counter. This car is one of few pre-war cars in this book with the correct original type of steering wheel, instead of the sprung four-spoke Brooklands wheel.

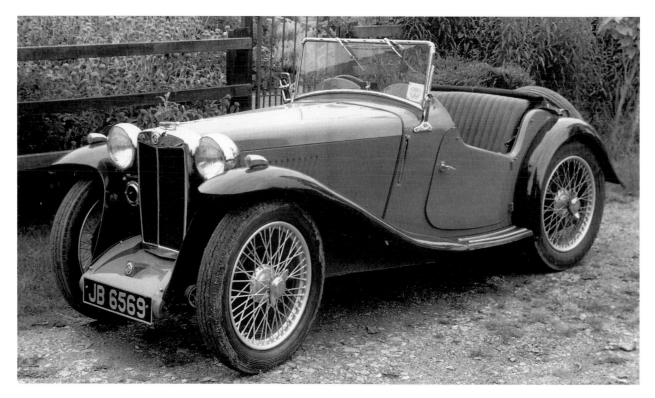

totally separate lines from the road cars, as we shall see in the next chapter, so there was no racing model in the P-type range. The car was not intended for first-rank competitions although P-types were used in events as different as trials and the Le Mans 24-hour race. While a supercharged P-type was not offered, some private owners fitted Marshall blowers, and some P-types were still supplied in chassis form for private owners who thought they could improve on Abingdon's standard offerings or who simply wanted something different. At least one P-type was bodied in Switzerland, with an elongated tail and a sloping radiator cowl.

The original P-type survived in production for about 18 months, the improved PB-type appearing in September 1935. To counter opposition from the bigger-engined Singer Nine Le Mans, the PB's engine was bored out to 60mm (RAC rated at 9hp) to give a capacity of 939cc, raising power output to 43.5bhp at 5500rpm. With slightly closer indirect gear ratios the new model had significantly better acceleration than the PA and was more flexible, although top speed was still around the 76mph mark. Another improvement was the Bishop Cam steering gear now fitted instead of the Marles Weller type. The PB was instantly recognisable from the front, as the radiator was fitted with painted slats, while on the dashboard a separate speedometer was

In 1935 the P-type became the PB, with a slatted radiator its distinguishing feature.

now fitted instead of the former central switch panel. Otherwise the car remained essentially the same and was offered with the three body styles – two-seater, four-seater and Airline coupé – at unchanged prices. For a while the 847cc PA-type continued to be available at the reduced price of £199 10s, seemingly in an effort to clear factory stock, and the last 27 PAs were modified to PB specification and given new chassis numbers.

Rated by many connoisseurs as the best and most practical of the overhead camshaft Midgets, the PB was destined for a short career, remaining in production for only nine months, with a production figure a quarter of the PA's. The integration of MG into the new Morris organisation signalled that there would be little future for the overhead camshaft models. The racing models had already gone by mid-1935 and the PB was being phased out during the spring of 1936, leaving the NB-type Magnette, for a few short months, as a legacy of Abingdon's overhead camshaft period. There was doubt in the minds of many enthusiasts about the form new MG sports cars might take, especially after the 1935 Motor Show introduction of the Two-litre saloon. Would the future scheme of things still include an MG Midget?

RACERS & RECORD-BREAKERS

No sooner, it seems, had the M-type appeared in production in 1929 than it was being entered in motor races. Its competition debut was in the Junior Car Club's high-speed trial at Brooklands in June 1929 where five M-types took part, including one driven by the Earl of March (later the Duke of Richmond and Gordon), and all won gold medals. There were further appearances at Brooklands as well as in trials throughout 1929, while in January 1930 F. M. Montgomery entered an M-type in the Monte Carlo Rally. He made fastest time of day in the 1100cc class at the Mont des Mules hillclimb at the end of the rally. In the Land's End trial held at Easter 1930, 30 M-types took part, and 18 of them were awarded the coveted gold medals.

At Abingdon, Reg Jackson had begun some experimental tuning work on the M-type's engine, an

Miss Victoria Worsley (and co-driver Foster) was a private entrant with her 12/12 M-type in the 1930 Double-Twelve race at Brooklands.

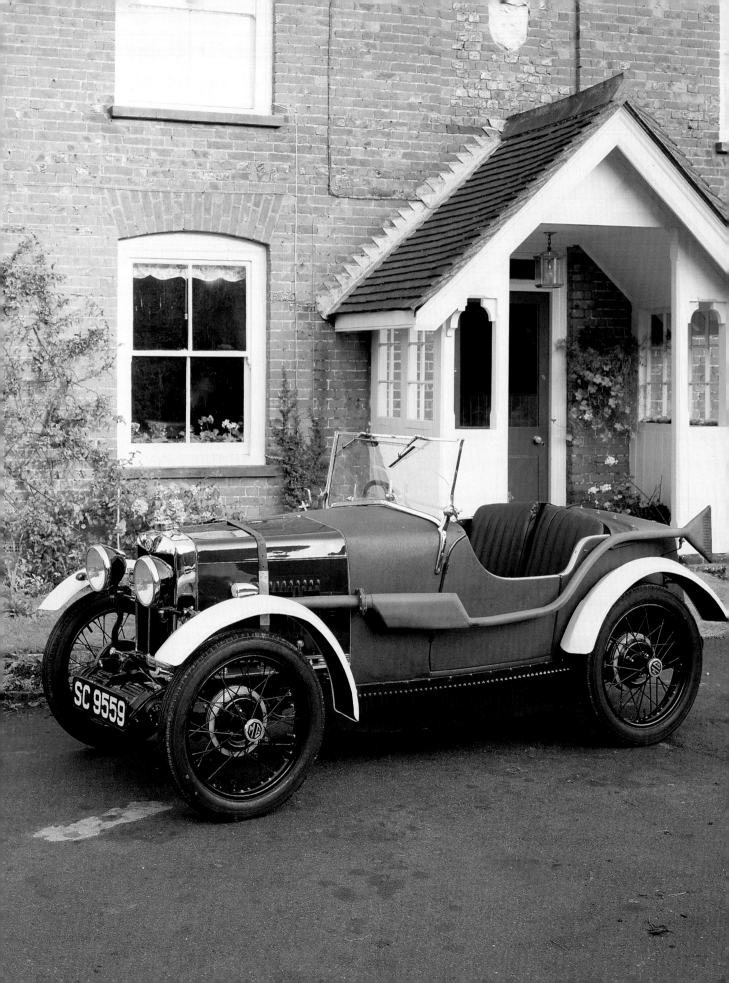

endeavour in which he was soon assisted by H. N. Charles. Charles designed a new camshaft which gave a small amount (7°) of overlap between the inlet valve opening and the exhaust valve closing and raised power output from 20 to 27bhp. When Kimber was approached by Cecil Randall and William Edmonson with the suggestion that they should run a team of three Midgets in the Double-Twelve Hour Race at Brooklands in May 1930, five specially-prepared Midgets were built with the tuned engines and modified bodywork, three for the Randall team known as 'The Tomato-Growers' and two for private entrants (Stisted/Black, Miss Worsley/Foster). A sixth M-type to standard specification was also entered, and though this one retired the five works-prepared cars finished third to seventh in the 1100cc class. Randall and Montgomery were best placed, also coming 14th overall, and 'The Tomato-Growers' took the team prize as well. This success prompted MG to offer a replica version of the race cars as the '12/12' model.

For the Le Mans 24-hour race in June 1930 two 12/12 models were entered, featuring further body modifications including 18-gallon petrol tanks. They were driven by F. H. B. (later Sir Francis) Samuelson with Freddie Kindell of MG, and R. C. Murton-Neale. with Jack Hicks. Neither car finished, both retiring with engine failure, but Samuelson, undeterred, got his engine rebuilt in time for the Belgian 24-hour race at Spa in

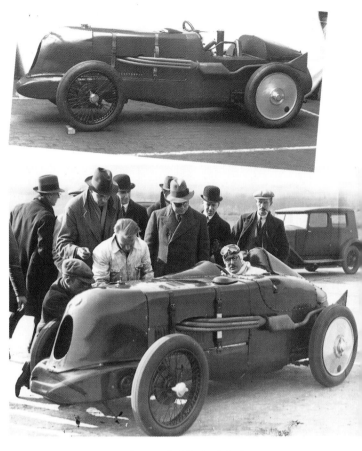

The first Midget record-breaker was EX120, here being prepared at Abingdon in 1931, still missing its cockpit fairing (top). At Brooklands in March 1931 (above), Eyston is at the wheel of EX120 while Eldridge (with the black eye-patch) stands by the side of the car. The mechanics – possibly Jackson and Phillips – seem to be performing some last-minute adjustment, with Cecil Cousins looking over their shoulders.

early July and although troubled by clutch slip in the later stages of the race finished fifth in class. There were further appearances by M-types in trials and races, while Samuelson, accompanied by his wife, took an M-type Sportsman's Coupé through the Monte Carlo Rally in January 1931. In another notable performance in May 1930 a works M-type was driven non-stop for almost eight hours to make 100 consecutive ascents of the Beggar's Roost trials hill in Devon.

During 1930 H. N. Charles was working on the new chassis design to replace the Morris Minor-derived frame when Kimber was approached by Jimmy Palmes, Captain George Eyston and Ernest Eldridge, who were looking for a suitable car for setting records in the 750cc class.

Of the M-type variations, 12/12 Replica was based on 1930 Brooklands team cars, and typically finished in distinctive brown and cream colours

(facing page). R. C. Murton-Neale and Jack Hicks drove this 12/12 M-type (above) in the 1930 Le Mans but retired with engine failure.

Kimber offered them the prototype chassis, dubbed EX120, and Eldridge developed a small-bore, short-stroke M–type engine (54×81mm, 742cc) fitted with a counter-balanced crankshaft. The car was fitted with a special streamlined body, featuring a cover over the passenger seat and a fairing behind the driver's head. EX120 was taken to the Montlhéry race track outside Paris where, on 30 December 1930, Eyston covered 100 kilometres (62 miles) at 87.3mph before a valve broke. This was quite promising but Kimber now wanted MG to be the first 750cc car to reach 100mph, a goal also chased by Austin. To this end, a leaf was taken out of Austin's book by fitting EX120 with a Powerplus supercharger. A hastily-made up radiator cowl was added

The lady in the hat is The Hon Mrs Chetwynd, so presumably this factory-fresh C-type (top left) is her car, C.0260, registered JO 2288, seen on the right at the front in the line-up of C-types (top right) before the start of the 1931 Double-Twelve Race. Next to it is C.0251, registered RX 8621, which won the race in the hands of the Earl of March and C. S. Staniland (above).

and Eyston took several records in February 1931 at speeds up to 103.13mph. In a further record attempt at Brooklands in March the engine blew up very comprehensively, but with a rebuilt engine the car was again taken to Montlhéry in September 1931 where Eyston took the one-hour record at 101mph though the

In June 1931 Sir Francis Samuelson and Freddie Kindell contested Le Mans for the second time in an MG, one of the new C-types, but were disqualified for taking too long to complete the last lap after a con rod had broken (right). Later in the 1931 season C-types were commonly raced with a supercharged engine but without the original radiator cowl. A happy Norman Black is seen on the lap of honour after winning the Ulster TT race (below).

car burst into flames on the last lap. Eyston managed to jump clear and escaped serious injury, being photographed with the burnt-out wreck afterwards.

At the celebrations after the February run, Kimber announced MG's intention to make a proper racing Midget in supercharged as well as unsupercharged form, and then proceeded to unveil the chassis of the first C-type. As it was planned to enter the new car in the Double-Twelve Hour Race at Brooklands in May, a hectic period followed to prepare no fewer than 14 of the new cars. Like EX120, the C-type had an under-750cc engine but used the standard bore of 57mm in conjunction with a much shorter stroke of 73mm to give 746cc. Valve timing was further improved to a 35°

overlap, which was subsequently adopted also for the road cars and used until 1936. The chassis was similar to that of the EX120 and the body was a doorless two-seater with deep cut-outs for entry and egress, two deep humps on the scuttle, a long pointed tail and, in original form, a cowled radiator. At first a supercharger was not fitted.

Thirteen C-types started in the Double-Twelve, in four teams of three cars each, with Hugh Hamilton driving the last car on his own. Among the team drivers were the Earl of March/C. S. Staniland, Norman Black/Fiennes, and two drivers who both later became leading MG racers: Ronnie Horton and Major A. T. Goldie Gardner. During the first day's race several of the MGs had problems with valve springs and broken pistons,

The C-type or Montlhéry Midget was a business-like little car, a Grand Prix car in miniature, ready for the road or race track. Together with the D-type, it was the first model to use H.N.Charles's new chassis design.

which led to many retirements including the Horton/Gardner car, but those that remained in the race built up an impressive lead. At the end of the second day five C-types finished the race in the first five places, with the Earl of March and Staniland first, Gibson/Fell second, Hamilton third, Parker/Cox fourth and Black/Fiennes in fifth place. The Earl of March's team, which had come first, fourth and fifth, also won the team prize. Rarely, if ever, has a new racing car had a more spectacular debut.

While MG was now beginning to accept orders from private owners for C-types, at £490 in standard form or £575 with a supercharger, there were further successes for the works-prepared cars. In the Saorstat Cup Race in Dublin, contested by small-capacity cars as part of the Irish Grand Prix, another gaggle of C-types came to the start, and Norman Black won the race, with Horton second and Gardner third. Black's performance on handicap was so outstanding that none of the bigger cars in the following day's Grand Prix could beat him, so he was also declared overall winner of the Irish Grand Prix. A week later two C-types were entered at Le Mans, where the Samuelson/Kindell car finished but was disqualified for having taken too long to complete the final lap.

The first race appearance for a blown C-type came in July, when Samuelson came fifth in class at the Grosser Preis von Deutschland at Nürburgring, but no less than nine blown C-types appeared in the Ulster TT on 22 August 1931 together with three unblown cars. Here

Norman Black repeated his victory in Dublin, beating an Alfa Romeo into second place, and Crabtree's C-type came third. In the last important fixture of the season, the 500-Mile Race at Brooklands in October, the best MG result was third place for E. R. Hall's specially-built single-seater C-type.

By then MG had also built a new record car. This was EX127, which achieved fame as the 'Magic Midget'. In comparison with EX120, a major difference was that the propshaft and differential were offset to the left, enabling a much lower seating position, but otherwise the chassis and engine were similar to those of the supercharged C-type. The body was a streamlined, long-tailed design with a much reduced cross section, and originally an external surface radiator was fitted. The car was first taken to Montlhéry in September 1931 – the fateful occasion when EX120 caught fire after taking the one-hour record. With Eyston temporarily in hospital after this mishap, Ernest Eldridge became the first driver to try out the new car, duly taking the five kilometres record at 110mph before the radiator burst.

Back at Abingdon a conventional internal radiator was fitted, and just before Christmas 1931 the car was ready, while Eyston had recovered sufficiently to be able to drive at Montlhéry again. The result was a further five records set at speeds over 114mph, yet the goal of two miles per minute remained elusive. In February 1932 a valiant attempt at the flying kilometre and flying mile records was made at Pendine Sands on the coast of South

The C-type dashboard was dominated by a soup-plate rev counter in front of the driver. The windscreen, here folded flat, was wire-mesh instead of glass.

Wales but 120mph remained just out of reach – Eyston's best recorded speed at this time was 119.48mph, with the required two-way average at 118.39mph. On its next outing, EX127 set a new class lap record at Brooklands, and also ran in the 500-Mile Race at Brooklands in September 1932, although it was forced to retire with a broken piston.

In December 1932 Eyston took EX127 to Montlhéry again, this time in company with one of the new J3 models. The J3 set up a new 24-hour class record, and EX127, which had been fitted with a cross-flow type cylinder head of the AB type found on the J-type, finally broke through the 120mph barrier, taking the kilometre and mile records at 120.56mph. Eyston and his mechanic Bert Denly then had a crack at the 12-hour record, which they just accomplished at 86.67mph, despite the rear main bearing fracturing towards the end of the run. In 1933 EX127 was fitted with a new J4 type engine and a new body of smaller cross section, but sadly for Eyston the new body was too small for him to fit in, and Bert Denly now took over the driving on his own. He was rewarded by a new set of records at Montlhéry in October 1933, at speeds up to 128.62mph, with the one-hour record at 110.87mph. Nor was this the car's farewell performance, for it was sold to German MG driver Bobby Kohlrausch, who had it fitted with a three-bearing Q-type engine in 1934. In this form the car broke the 130mph barrier at Gyon in Hungary in 1935. Kohlrausch next had a special bronze cylinder head made which

ultimately resulted in the engine delivering 146bhp at 7500rpm with blower pressure at 39lb/sq in, and in October 1936 on the Frankfurt Autobahn Kohlrausch raised the flying mile record in the 750cc class to 140.6mph while the officials and other bystanders sensibly covered up their ears! In between record runs, Kohlrausch used the car for a variety of races and hillclimbs in Germany, fitted with an alternative body. The Magic Midget was finally acquired by Mercedes-Benz, who were anxious to study an engine which had given such amazing performance for its size, and it is thought that the car was scrapped or destroyed at Stuttgart during the war. Kimber claimed that the engine was used as the inspiration for the 1939 Mercedes-Benz 1.5-litre V8 engine built for the Tripoli Grand Prix.

While EX127 went from strength to strength, Midgets on the race tracks were not to equal that first sensational 1931 season – mainly because race officials steadily increased the handicap speeds for the Midget class after each MG success. A new cross-flow cylinder head with twin carburettors was fitted to C-types for the 1000-Mile Race at Brooklands in 1932, where the highest-placed C-type was the Norman Black/Gibson car in third place. The race produced a rare MG tragedy as H. Leeson was killed when his C-type crashed. At Le Mans the Samuelson/Norman Black C-type retired with a leaking fuel tank, but Hamilton got a class win in the German Grand Prix. The Tourist Trophy produced a host of MG retirements, only two C-types finishing

Even before the sad demise of EX120 a new record-breaker had been built – EX127 or the Magic Midget. Captain

George Eyston poses in the car while mechanic and sometime driver Bert Denly holds the cockpit fairing.

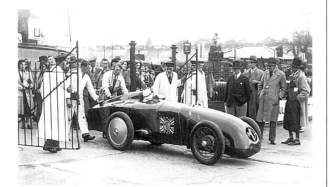

The Magic Midget was used not only for record-breaking but also the occasional race meetings at Brooklands. This is Eyston being pushed on to the track on Whit Monday 1932.

The Magic Midget never went more slowly than when mounted on this float, MG's entry in the procession through Abingdon marking King George V's Silver Jubilee in 1935.

The Magic Midget was eventually re-bodied with a nose similar to the R-type's, and was painted white when it was sold to the German driver Bobby Kohlrausch. In this form the car was used for continental hill-climbs, but Kohlrausch re-fitted the original streamlined body for his later record runs.

although E. R. Hall managed third place. At the end of this otherwise disappointing season Ronnie Horton won the 500-Mile Race at Brooklands (with Norman Black in sixth place) to provide some compensation. Horton's car was a rather special C-type fitted with an off-set single-seater body, and he later used it to set several long-distance class records at Brooklands.

From 1933 onwards MG's racing efforts were mostly centred on the new K3 Magnette model, but the Midgets were not completely neglected. While the J-types had been launched in mid-1932, the racing versions, J3 and J4, followed rather later – the J4 only in March 1933. The J3 was broadly speaking a supercharged 746cc version of the J2, while the J4 was a more specialised racing model with a larger supercharger, a doorless body, and bigger 12in brake drums borrowed from the Magna/Magnette models. The J3 was a versatile car, capable of taking in events as different as Le Mans and the Monte Carlo Rally. Its finest hour came at Montlhéry in December 1932 when one took all the 750cc class records from 12 to 24 hours, complementing the EX127 record run. The J4 was an extraordinarily potent little machine in the right hands – mostly those of Hugh Hamilton. He took delivery of the first J4 and went to Germany, taking a number of class wins at the Eifel Rennen and in various hillclimbs. Meanwhile, to prove that there was still some life left in the C-type, Ludovic Ford and Maurice Baumer drove a C-type to a class win at Le Mans, finishing sixth overall and second on the Index of Performance.

At the Mannin Beg race on the Isle of Man in July 1933 all six K3 Magnettes retired, mostly with a variety of mechanical failures. This left the MG honour to be defended by the J4s, of which the D. K. Mansell car came second, Ford/Baumer following in third place. Yet in many ways the most notable J4 result was Hamilton's *second* place in the 1933 Tourist Trophy race, at an average speed of 73.46mph. A bungled pit-stop delayed Hamilton by seven minutes half-way through the race, and he had to stop again for petrol on the penultimate lap, but he lost by only 40 seconds to Nuvolari's K3 Magnette.

The J4 was replaced in 1934 by the Q-type. The new model's engine was based on the three-bearing P-type unit, and a hefty Zoller supercharger was fitted. The wheelbase was lengthened to the same as the K3's, and N-type axles were fitted. A Wilson pre-selector gearbox was fitted, and the body was similar to the later pointed-tail 1934 K3 model. The leading Q-type driver was Bill Everitt, who several times in the course of 1934 set new lap records and standing kilometre/mile records at Brooklands. Yet major racing successes eluded the Q-type. There were probably two reasons for this: first, race handicappers had got wise to the potential of the MG Midget and were setting unrealistic targets for the car to beat; and second, the Q-type was difficult to drive and keep under control, being prone to wheelspin and generally too fast for its chassis. On the bumpy surface of Brooklands a Q-type ride was an uncomfortable experience, the car being in the air quite as much as it

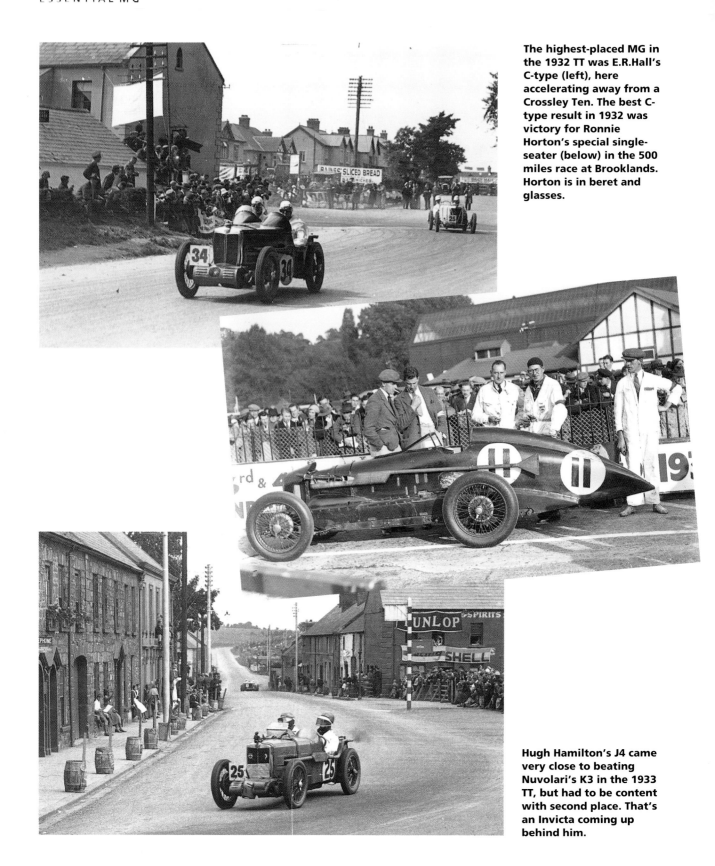

The highest-placed MG in the 1932 TT was E.R.Hall's C-type (left), here accelerating away from a Crossley Ten. The best C-type result in 1932 was victory for Ronnie Horton's special single-seater (below) in the 500 miles race at Brooklands. Horton is in beret and glasses.

Hugh Hamilton's J4 came very close to beating Nuvolari's K3 in the 1933 TT, but had to be content with second place. That's an Invicta coming up behind him.

'Leonides' was originally one of the 1935 PA Le Mans team cars, but was rebodied in this form in the USA by the Collier **brothers, who took the car back to Le Mans in 1939 and also raced it extensively in their own country.**

was on the track! Still, Kenneth Evans managed a third place in the Nuffield Trophy Race at Donington in September 1934 in his Q-type.

There was nothing wrong with the Q-type engine, however, and H. N. Charles decided to tackle the problem by designing a new chassis for it. He came up with one of the most remarkable racing car chassis designs of the 1930s, incorporating fully independent front and rear suspension by wishbones and torsion bars. The actual frame design was a lightweight yet highly rigid Y-shaped box section, weighing a mere 57lb, with the Q-type engine and pre-selector gearbox installed in the fork of the Y. Another departure from normal practice was that the new car, known as the R-type, was designed only as a single-seater, with a streamlined body in which the radiator, supercharger and front suspension were neatly tucked away behind the same cowl. The weight of a complete R-type was 12½cwt and when the car was revealed to the public in April 1935 MG quoted a price of £750.

In its original form the R-type was scarcely fully developed, and the suspension geometry, with roll centre at ground level, caused the car to assume distinctly non-Anglo Saxon attitudes as it went through corners, much to the dismay of drivers. In its debut race, the

International Trophy Race at Brooklands in May 1935, an R-type won its class, and although R-types were often handicapped or eliminated by teething troubles during their short racing career, they still performed impressively well at times – both in France, where R-types were run by the Menier team, and in England, where brother-and-sister Kenneth and Doreen Evans of Bellevue Garage were among the R-type's most important exponents, benefiting from a special twin overhead camshaft cylinder head developed by Michael McEvoy. Will Handley, Bill Everitt and George Eyston also all drove R-types.

Time, however, had run out on the R-type. In July 1935, at the time of the Morris Motors takeover, MG withdrew from racing and sold the remaining competition cars. The events of that summer also spelled the end of any plans for adoption of the R-type's advanced engineering in road cars. But before the axe fell on MG competition activities, June 1935 saw an unusually determined onslaught on Le Mans, where a team of three PA Midgets, managed by George Eyston, was entered – perhaps with one eye on the biennial Rudge-Whitworth trophy, for which MG would qualify as the lone PA of Madame Itier and Druck had finished 17th in the 1934 race. Eyston's 1935 team was chiefly remarkable for the fact that all six drivers were women, Doreen Evans among them, and although they got nowhere near the biennial cup they all ran like clockwork to finish in 24th, 25th and 26th place overall. P-types ran again at Le Mans in 1937, 1938 and 1939,

In 1935, the year MG withdrew from competition, George Eyston acted as team manager (and chaperone?) for the all-ladies team with their three PAs at Le Mans. From left are Barbara Skinner, Doreen Evans, Margaret Simpson, Eyston, Joan Richmond, Barbara Eaton and Margaret Allan.

Doreen Evans, with Kenneth Evans and Wilkie Wilkinson, walking their Q-type in the paddock at Brooklands.

Launched in 1934, the Q-type looked very effective but achieved no major racing successes.

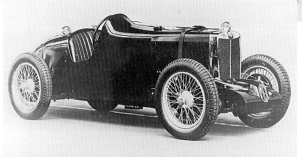

one of the final pre-war entries being the American PA-based 'Leonides' special of Miles Collier – who with co-driver Lewis Welch had to retire with a burst fuel tank after eight hours.

The only form of competition in which MG continued to play an active part in the late 1930s was trials, where the factory supported two teams, the 'Cream Crackers' and the 'Three Musketeers'. The Musketeer cars were Magnettes but the Cream Crackers used

The Evans R-type at Donington Park. Doreen is relaxing on the pit counter, but Wilkie Wilkinson and Kenneth Evans look rather tense.

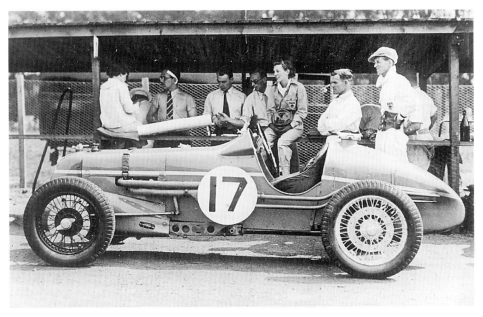

Here is an R-type further afield, in the Coppa Acerbo race at Pescara, Italy.

The R-type's racing debut came in the Junior Car Club's International Trophy Race at Brooklands in May 1935. There are four R-types here, with Eyston's at the front.

Midgets, drivers Toulmin, Bastock and MacDermid starting out with PAs in 1934. In 1935 MG built three supercharged PBs for the Cream Cracker team, where Maurice Toulmin was now joined by new recruits 'Jesus' Jones and Ken Crawford. These cars, together with the Magnettes of the Musketeers team, competed with great success throughout 1936, winning the MCC trials championship, and were eventually replaced by trials versions of the new TA Midget.

FROM TA TO TC

The integration of The MG Car Company Limited into Morris Motors Limited – or what would soon be called the Nuffield Organisation – was a process with several stages: first, the appointment of Leonard Lord as managing director of MG (as well as Morris) on 1 July 1935, with Cecil Kimber demoted to general manager; next, on 10 July 1935, the formal transfer of the MG shares from Morris Industries Limited (Lord Nuffield's personal investment company) to Morris Motors Limited; and, later in the same month, the famous statement which announced the end of MG racing cars and of the company's participation in motor sport. In October 1935 the first of a new generation of MG cars was introduced at the London Motor Show: the SA or Two-litre saloon, which made extensive use of

Introduced in 1936, the TA was instantly recognisable as an MG Midget, but was a little bigger all round. The two-tone colours often seen on previous models were replaced by single colours, with the slats of the radiator grille often painted to match the interior trim.

mechanical components from the Morris/Wolseley range. It was the first MG production model to feature pushrod-operated overhead valves rather than an overhead camshaft, and the first to have Lockheed hydraulic brakes. It was slow to go into production and it was spring 1936 before SAs began to reach customers.

The next new MG was introduced in June 1936. This was the replacement for the PB, a new Midget which was to be called the Series T and which was hailed by

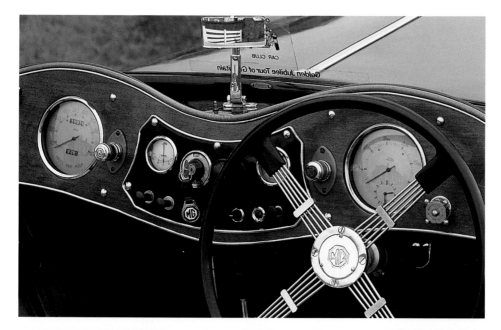

The dashboard was redesigned for the TA, with the speedometer now in front of the passenger, and a combined instrument and switch panel in the centre.

The TA engine with its pushrod-operated overhead valves was derived from the contemporary Wolseley 10/40 engine – the cylinder head casting is actually stamped '10W&M'. The electrical equipment was grouped on one side...

...while both inlet and exhaust manifolds were on the other, with the bulky air cleaner tucked away at the rear to fit in the limited space under the bonnet.

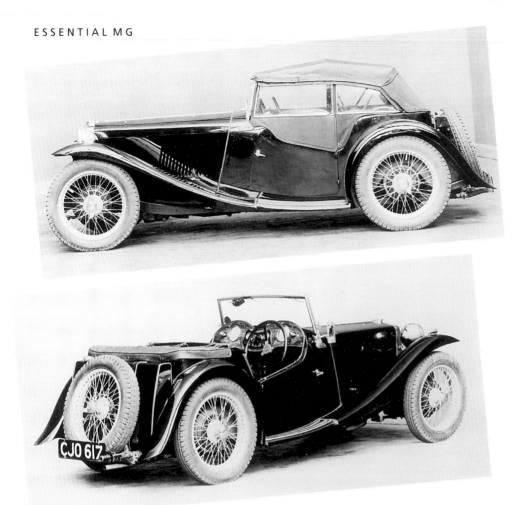

This car is the prototype TA photographed at Cowley in June 1936. The most noticeable difference compared with later production models is that the trafficators are built into the scuttle, P-type style. From the rear it displays its narrow rear wings and wide petrol tank, both modified in early 1937, and also the tiny tubular rear lamp that was soon replaced by a larger round lamp and eventually by the familiar D-shape lamp.

The Autocar with the headline 'The Midget Grows Up'. To the casual observer there could be no doubt that the new car was, indeed, an MG. Its shape was so like the PB, with only a few detail differences, and the radiator with its centre bar, false nosepiece and painted slats was instantly recognisable. But the new model was in fact appreciably larger than its predecessor. At 7ft 10in, the wheelbase was some 7in longer than on a PB, and within 2in of the N-type Magnette. Overall length was similarly increased, and the car was 2cwt heavier than a P-type (although still 3cwt lighter than the overweight N-type Magnette). The engine had a capacity of 1292cc and was RAC rated at 10hp, a considerable step up from the 939cc and 9hp of the PB, as well as topping the N-type's six-cylinder engine of 1271cc (and 12hp).

More importantly, the MPJG-type engine of the T-series was nothing more or less than the simple pushrod unit from the Wolseley 10/40 saloon, a four-cylinder which was a close relative of the Morris Ten's sidevalve engine. These engines were part of the extended Morris engine family, whose common trademark was a 102mm stroke, an extraordinary dimension by MG Midget standards, almost 20mm longer than the 83mm stroke found on all previous road models from M to PB. The long stroke would prove to be the Achilles heel of the T-series – or TA-series – engine. The engine developed 50bhp, a reasonable increase over the 40bhp or so which the same engine gave in single-carburettor form in the Wolseley 10/40 saloon, and at peak power it turned at 4500rpm. This was 1000rpm less than the PA/PB engines, yet the TA's piston speed was higher because of the longer stroke. In terms of actual power output, the TA gave almost 10bhp more than the PB.

There was nothing unconventional about the engine, and one benefit at least of having abandoned the overhead camshaft was that the TA became rather more mechanic-friendly, while the persistent problem of oil leaking into the dynamo was now a thing of the past. The clutch was cork-lined and ran in oil, as was established Morris practice. The four-speed gearbox was a standard Morris/Wolseley design, initially without synchromesh, but this was added after 183 engines had been made, so from August 1936 top and third gears were fitted with synchromesh, and at the same time the

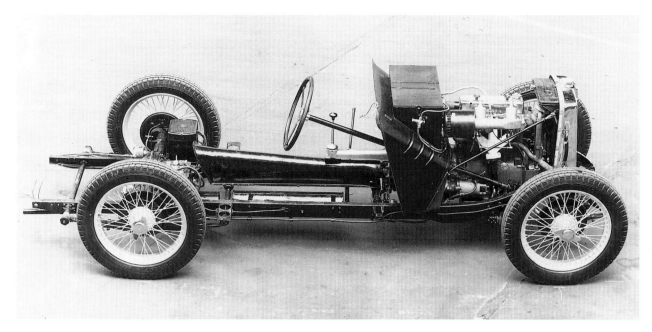

indirect gear ratios became slightly higher and closer. A remote control gearchange was still fitted, but with a standard mushroom or pear shaped gear lever knob instead of an octagonal one. The entire power unit was mounted on rubber, which undoubtedly reduced vibration but also made the chassis rather less rigid.

The chassis itself was broadly speaking in line with well-established MG tradition. The side members were partially boxed in at the front alongside the engine, and there were five tubular crossmembers. A centralised chassis lubrication system with grouped nipples under the bonnet was introduced in 1938. The chassis side members went under the rear axle, and both front and back springs were mounted in sliding trunnions at their rear ends. Bishop Cam steering gear was used, but a novelty on an MG Midget was the Lockheed hydraulic braking system, with 9in drums front and rear. The handbrake was of the fly-off type.

As originally introduced the TA was offered with only one standard body, an open two-seater, and although its lines followed the P-types closely it was rather larger and roomier than any previous Midget, with interior dimensions greater even than the Magnette – particularly in terms of width, and headroom when the hood was raised. Here at last was a Midget which was not designed for midgets, a small MG in which drivers of even above average size could feel comfortable. The standard steering wheel had three solid spokes and was covered in black plastic material, but many cars were fitted with the sprung four-spoke Brooklands type wheel.

The TA chassis was really just like the earlier Midgets, with parallel side members underslung at the back and tubular crossmembers.

The column, initially not adjustable, was given telescopic adjustment in 1938. The wood veneer facia had a rev counter in front of the driver and speedometer in front of the passenger, with a centre panel for other instruments and minor controls.

It is unlikely that very many enthusiasts regretted the absence of a TA four-seater – the small Midget-based four-seaters had always been of limited practicality, and the MG enthusiast in search of an open four-seater would soon be offered a more practical (if less sporting) alternative in the shape of the VA 1½-litre four-seater which became available in early 1937. It is, however, a matter of regret that only two TA chassis were fitted with the pretty Airline coupé body. Undoubtedly one reason why the Airline was dropped was that this body was built by Carbodies, and as a member of the Morris group of companies MG was now expected to source most of its body requirements from Morris Bodies Branch in Coventry, from where the TA two-seater came. Not many TAs were supplied in chassis form; the factory records suggest there were only 11 such deliveries, of which 10 were exported to Australia where they were fitted with locally-made coachwork very similar to the standard two-seater.

There were still a few special-bodied cars. Lord Ashley, an enthusiastic MG Car Club member, had a TA

bodied – or at least substantially modified – by Offord, featuring fully skirted front wings with the headlamps partially built into the wing valances, and smaller than normal wheels with large-section tyres. This car was also fitted with a 1.5-litre engine VA engine. Another car was built in Denmark although it appears to have been shipped from Abingdon with standard coachwork. The Danish MG importer commissioned the body from the coachbuilder Jensen of Højer, the result being a two-seater drophead coupé with an enclosed compartment for two spare wheels in the elongated tail. Pretty in a Teutonic manner but appearing tail-heavy, the car was supplied to a Danish nobleman and was still in existence in the late 1970s, when regrettably its owner decided to replace the special body with a replica of the standard two-seater. A third car which happily still exists is the Park Ward TA, built by the owner of Park Ward just after World War Two. This was another drophead coupé, with specially-designed, bulbous front wings, matching rear wings with spats, and a roomy boot within the swept tail. It seems originally to have had the standard TA radiator but was at some stage fitted with a cowl, and in its present restored form has a cut-down Y-type

The TB is difficult to distinguish externally from the TA. The only clue, not visible here, is that the bulge over the dynamo on the left-hand side of the bonnet is a little lower, but it is a very different story under the bonnet. The all-new short-stroke XPAG engine was to power all subsequent MG Midgets.

radiator. It had several luxury features of which the most unusual – in 1946! – was electric windows. The car has been beautifully restored by its present owner who lives in the Netherlands.

An alternative standard body was introduced in 1938. This was the Tickford drophead coupé, following on

The Abingdon assembly
lines were busy in 1937
as never before,
production being
dominated by the SA
saloon as well as the TA
Midget.

from the Tickford drophead bodies which were by then available on the SA and VA chassis. 'Tickford', originally the name of a particular style of all-weather body built by Salmons and Sons of Newport Pagnell, had by 1938 become the name for Salmons' drophead coupé style, although then and later the name Tickford was widely used to refer to the coachbuilding company itself. On the TA chassis, the Tickford body was a cosy and civilised alternative to the two-seater. The prototype had a rather bulbous tail enclosing the fuel tank but the production model introduced in August 1938 had the standard TA's exposed slab tank. Full-height doors with wind-down windows were fitted, there were well-upholstered bucket seats instead of the bench type seat seen on the two-seater, and the interior was fully carpeted. The scuttle was flat and the dashboard rather differently shaped, though fitted with the standard instrumentation. The windscreen frame was fixed but the windscreen itself was hinged at the top and could be opened. The hood was a work of art, with a mohair outer cover and fully lined; it incorporated a letterbox-slit glass rear window and even an interior lamp. As well as folding back fully, it could be left in the intermediate 'de ville' position, with the side cant rails folded back and the front part of the hood rolled up. The downside of all this luxury was that the Tickford weighed 2cwt more than the two-seater. It also cost £269 10s when the two-seater was available for only

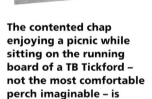

THE MG MIDGET Series TB

SAFETY FAST!

The contented chap enjoying a picnic while sitting on the running board of a TB Tickford – not the most comfortable perch imaginable – is

MG's publicity manager George Tuck, a keen amateur photographer whose work was often used in MG sales brochures.

£222, but it found a ready market and about 20% of Midgets were fitted with the Tickford body in 1938-39.

When early TAs became available for road test in late 1936 the new model turned out to offer a slight but definite improvement over the PB in terms of performance, with a genuine 80mph top speed and

The Tickford drophead coupé, available on the TB chassis as well as on the TA shown here, was a more luxurious alternative to the two-seater.

The Tickford hood was fitted with external hood irons, and could be folded half-way back to the 'de ville' position. Together with the wind-down glass side windows, it gave good weather protection.

The Tickford TA's inviting interior, with individual seats and full carpeting. The dashboard is tucked away under the flat scuttle.

quicker acceleration – in fact TA performance was nearly comparable to that of the N-type of all but identical engine size. The car was found to be more comfortable, quieter and more flexible than earlier Midgets, but also a little 'softer' in character, the suspension less firm, the steering a little heavier. Petrol consumption was of the order of 28–33mpg.

With a total production of just over 3000 cars from 1936 to 1939, the TA was the most popular Midget since the M-type, while at the same time MG's output was usefully boosted by the popularity of the SA and VA models, making 1937 the best individual pre-war year, with 2901 cars made, record sales of almost £700,000 and a net operating profit of over £25,000. MG was fortunate in that there were very few other small sports cars on the market at this time, Singer, Riley and Triumph having all pulled out of the sports car market by then. The nearest competitor was the new Morgan 4-4, which offered 78mph performance from an 1122cc Coventry-Climax engine for £194 in two-seater form, with four-seater and drophead coupé alternatives becoming available, but it took Morgan until 1950 to turn out little more than 1400 of these cars. Production of the HRG was on an even more limited scale, and while their 1100cc model would out-perform a TA it cost £289; the more common 1500cc model, which could do 85mph, cost £395. The Rapier had started life as a small Lagonda and continued in production after Lagonda's 1935 receivership, made by a separate company. Its specification was delicious, with twin overhead camshafts for the 1100cc engine and a pre-selector gearbox, but at £270 in chassis form (most complete cars cost £350-£400) the Rapier was too

expensive and the last of some 300 cars were built in 1937. Technically interesting was the front-wheel drive BSA Scout, but its 1200cc sidevalve engine and three-speed gearbox with dashboard-mounted lever added up to an unsporting specification, and 70mph was the limit for any Scout. Yet at £159 10s for a two-seater it was attractively priced, and even the four-seater coupé version cost only £196.

It would be many years before there was any serious competition for the MG Midget. In the spring of 1939 the TA was replaced by an improved model, the TB-series. While the chassis and bodywork were hardly changed, the TB had an all-new and much better engine, a 1250cc unit of 66.5×90mm developing 54.4bhp at 5200rpm. This was the first of the XPAG engines, destined to become famous in the post-war period, and was based on the XPJM 1140cc engine introduced in the new Morris Ten Series M at the 1938 Motor Show and

All of the TC's salient features are revealed in this beautifully executed cutaway, drawn by Chris Plant for *Classic Cars* magazine.

CHRIS PLANT
classic

Things never changed much at Abingdon: this is the assembly area in the late 1940s, with Y-types as well as TCs, the latter mostly carrying Nuffield Exports stickers on their windscreens.

also fitted in a new Wolseley Ten in early 1939. Compared with the basic Morris/Wolseley engine, the MG version was bored out so the RAC rating was now 11hp. A 12mm shorter stroke than the TA engine meant lower piston speeds – this and a new fully counter-balanced crankshaft made for a notably more robust unit than its predecessor, and one that was also more susceptible to tuning. The transmission was revised too. There was a single dry-plate Borg & Beck clutch, the gearbox had synchromesh on second and closer gear ratios, and the final drive ratio was lowered to improve low-speed acceleration.

Prices were slightly increased, to £225 for the two-seater and £270 for the drophead coupé. No full road test was ever carried out but the TB is likely to have had very similar performance to the TA, with slightly better acceleration. Its career was cut short by the outbreak of war, and only 379 TBs had been made by the time MG's car assembly lines were closed for the duration in October 1939, although some cars remained available in stock and exports continued into 1940. The company's own demonstrator, CJB 59, which was tried by *The Autocar* in June 1940, was quietly tucked away in a corner of the factory.

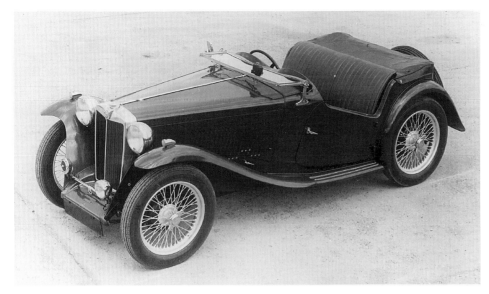

A fold-flat windscreen was standard on the TC, as indeed on all Midgets from the J-type to the TF. It was up to private owners to fit their own aeroscreens – desirable for motoring with the screen folded unless one wore goggles.

A group of six TCs in Langham Place, London, on their way to the Motor Industry Golden Jubilee Cavalcade in Regent's Park in 1946. According to the sign on its windscreen, the car on the left was destined for New York afterwards.

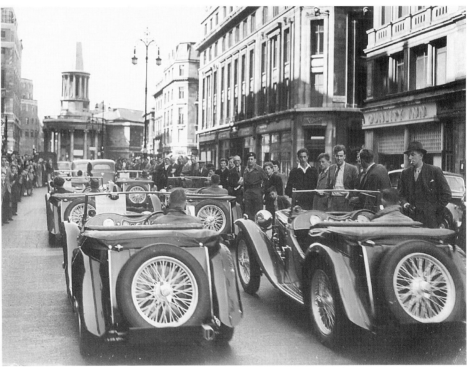

It was nearly six years before an MG car was manufactured again. Although it had been the intention to launch a new small MG saloon with the XPAG engine in 1940, the prototype for the MG 'Ten' also had to spend the war years in storage, and even afterwards the new model was slow to emerge, launched as the One-and-a-Quarter litre (Series Y) in the spring of 1947. Although there were various plans within the Nuffield Organisation for ambitious new MG sports cars – not to mention the MG version of the Morris Minor – in 1945 the men of Abingdon wanted to get back into car production as quickly as possible, so they dusted off the old TB demonstrator. With a few changes, this became the prototype for a new MG sports car, the TC. Most importantly, the body was widened by 4in between the rear door pillars. The traditional sliding trunnions for the road springs were replaced by shackles, with the springs mounted in rubber bushes, and improved Luvax-Girling shock absorbers were fitted. The two six-volt batteries mounted in battery boxes under the tonneau area were replaced by a single 12-volt battery in a box on the scuttle. There were other small improvements, and a big improvement in the price, which was now £375 basic, or £480 including Purchase Tax, when the new model

The cast-aluminium rocker cover was fitted to about 900 TCs in 1946-47, but may also be seen on earlier or later cars. The arrangement of the carburettors and air filter is the same as on the TB.

The typical T-type interior, from a TC, with a single backrest and two separate cushions . Apart from beige, the interior trim could also be red or green, all three colours being offered on a black car.

Like the TA and TB, the TC originally had a wood veneer dashboard , although it was changed to a Rexine covering in 1948. The grab handle and the Brooklands steering wheel are extras.

The arrangement of a single horn and fog lamp on this TC's badge bar is characteristic of all early T-types (facing page).

was introduced to the public in October 1945.

The early cars were all black, with a choice of red, green or biscuit trim, but gradually a wider choice of colours was reintroduced, including green, red, blue and cream. By the end of 1945 81 TCs had been built, but production quickly gathered pace and in the best year, 1948, more than 3000 cars were made. This was the period when Britain's motor industry was exhorted to export as many cars as possible, and 23 TCs were shipped abroad in 1945; in 1948 just over 90% of production was earmarked for export destinations. By then a small miracle had occurred: the Americans had begun buying

MG sports cars. A first batch of 20 TCs had been shipped to New York in 1946, and a further 1800 cars would follow over the next three years. Other British cars were being exported to the USA, mostly small saloons such as the Austin A40, which for a time sold in far greater numbers than the MG Midget. Apart from the Crosley there was no small domestic American car on the market, nor yet any sports car, so the small British cars did find a niche in the market, selling to the customer in search of something different – which the MG most certainly was compared with the average American car. It was not a cheap alternative: in 1949 a TC cost around $1850 in

A distinctly non-standard effect was achieved by Miss Chili Williams, an American pin-up model who had her TC finished in polka dots to match her bathing suit.

New York, or about the same as a Ford or Chevrolet convertible – domestic sedans were around $1400.

The sudden popularity of the TC in the USA forced MG to bring out a version of the car which was specially tailored to the needs of this market. Left-hand drive was not available but in other respects the EX-U version of the TC was more suited to American motoring conditions. It had front and rear bumpers, twin stop/tail lamps and flashing indicators at a time when the standard Midget was not even equipped with trafficators. The windscreen was made of laminated glass, twin windtone horns were mounted under the bonnet, and there were

other smaller modifications. As far as can be ascertained from the not very detailed factory records, the EX-U model went into production in late 1948 and barely 500 of these cars were made before TC production ceased a year later.

Another way of making export sales, especially to markets with restrictive tariffs or other forms of import control, was to send cars abroad in the form of CKD (Completely Knocked Down) kits which were then assembled, typically with some local content, in the destination country. The first market to take MG cars in this form was Eire, where some 84 TCs were assembled

Two colourful pages from the TC sales brochure, one bravely showing the car with hood and sidescreens in place, the other appealing to sporting instincts with the windscreen folded flat. The '10.9' legend on the number plates refers to the taxable (or RAC) horsepower imposed in Britain until 1947. These delightful renderings are more true to scale than most of those found in the pre-war brochures...

from CKD kits between 1947-49 by Messrs Booth Poole and Co Ltd in Dublin. There were also 10 TCs supplied in chassis form but it is not known where these ended up, or what bodies were fitted on them – although presumably one was the basis for George Phillips' 1949 Le Mans car.

The TC was not greatly modified during its four-year production run, but a number of small changes were introduced at various points in the early part of 1948 which together contributed to giving a significant difference in appearance between an 'early' and a 'late' TC. The changes included a new type of foglamp, the reintroduction of red engine paint (early post-war engines were painted grey) together with a body-coloured instead of a black bulkhead, a fawn instead of a black tonneau cover, a one-piece instead of a split rear window in the hood, and a Rexine-covered facia board with a metallic tan switch panel instead of the walnut veneer facia with a black switch panel. There were also slight changes to the seats, and the door panels were trimmed in Rexine on the later cars instead of leather.

Precisely 10,000 TCs had been made (apart from the prototype) by the time production of the model ceased in November 1949. This was a production figure three times as large as those achieved by the most popular pre-war models, and by the time TC production came to an end the MG name had become known throughout the

world. MG was also still largely without competition in its sector of the market. In late 1949 the TC cost £528 (including Purchase Tax) compared with the £557 charged for a Morgan 4/4 or £576 for a Singer Nine roadster, while both the 1100cc and the 1500cc HRG cost over £1000. While post-war road tests of the TC suggested a top speed of 75-78mph, these slightly lower than pre-war figures may have been attributable to the inferior quality 'Pool' petrol then available, and were certainly enough to comfortably out-perform the Singer (which struggled to reach 65mph) and equal the (estimated) 75mph of the Morgan, while almost reaching the 80mph offered by the HRG 1500. At the time there were hardly any other small-capacity sports cars available anywhere in the world – if one disregards the two dozen or so Volkswagen-based cars which had come out of Austria, bringing renewed attention to the famous name of Porsche...

FROM TD TO TF

By 1949 the TC was beginning to seem a little old-fashioned. No matter that there were no other new post-war designs on the market in the popular sports car class, virtually all British car makers had brought out up-to-date models with features such as independent front suspension, although some had held out until the first post-war London Motor Show in 1948 – including MG's own parent company, Morris. After this event, apart from the Fords, the MG TC was virtually the only model of 1936 design still in production. Within the Nuffield Organisation, the Morris, Riley and Wolseley ranges were all new post-war introductions, as was MG's own Y-type saloon, which although designed in 1939-40 incorporated advanced features such as independent front suspension and rack-and-pinion steering.

The time had come to do something about a new MG sports car. The question was, should Abingdon be

Only the very early TDs like this car had solid rather than pierced **wheels, and also a sloping line to the top of the front sidescreens.**

left to do their own, or should the new car be developed by the Morris engineers at Cowley? There was also at this time a question mark over whether MG should continue to produce sports cars at all. One of the more radical solutions called for both the TC and the Y-type to be phased out and Abingdon given over to production of an MG version of the Morris Minor, with a four-door body, a traditional MG front and a new overhead camshaft engine of 1100cc. The stylists even produced mock-ups of MG saloons based on the Morris Oxford/Six design. While the Morris Minor design was still in the melting pot, it was suggested that Morris should continue to produce the Morris Eight, and the Minor should be put into small-scale production at Abingdon to test the

Taken straight from the assembly line to be photographed in the studio at Cowley, this TD displays the left-hand drive option offered for the first time on an MG sports car.

market for this new concept of a small car. However, when the dust had settled and the Minor was safely in production at Cowley, the engineers and stylists there developed a small two-seater sports car which undoubtedly would have incorporated many Minor components and was probably based on the floorpan of the Minor's unitary construction body. Power would most likely have been provided by the still-born 1100cc overhead camshaft engine.

Although mock-ups of the project with all-enveloping streamlined bodies were photographed on a number of occasions between 1947 and 1951, and although a longer-wheelbase four-seater version would eventually contribute to the MG ZA Magnette design, the sports car remained stillborn – perhaps because Nuffield could not afford to develop and produce the car, perhaps because there was uncertainty about whether the market wanted a modern MG. For the time being the Cowley engineers let MG be, and instead Abingdon's own modernisation of the Midget went ahead, on the proverbial shoestring budget.

Syd Enever and his colleagues in the small engineering department at Abingdon looked at the Y-type with interest, for although their old boss H. N. Charles had designed an MG with fully-independent suspension almost 15 years earlier in the shape of the R-type, the Y-type was the first production MG to have independent suspension. This was a wishbone and coil spring layout originally designed by a young suspension specialist at Cowley, Alec Issigonis, and intended for the

Morris Ten, but when it turned out to be too expensive for a Morris it was fitted to the MG instead. In the autumn of 1948 the men at Abingdon took a Y-type chassis, cut the wheelbase from 8ft 3in to the TC dimension of 7ft 10in, and put a TC body on top. This was broadly speaking the TD prototype, though there was to be rather more to it than that as development progressed. Where both the TC and the Y-type had the chassis underslung at the rear, the new Midget chassis swept over the rear axle to provide the increased suspension movement desirable in many export territories. The body was extensively redesigned. The engine was modified but was still basically the same XPAG engine as had served in the TB and TC. Front suspension and steering gear were largely identical to the Y-type's, front and rear track dimensions were the same as on the saloon, and 15in disc wheels replaced the 19in wire wheels found on the earlier T-series.

This last feature probably caused MG enthusiasts more anguish than any other! Other than that they were happy to embrace the improved road-holding, handling and comfort of the new model. Many of the improvements on the TD were dictated by the requirements of the American market, now including bumpers as standard on all models, improved brakes with

A TD on test with *Road & Track* magazine in the USA, a market of immense importance to MG after the war – 79 per cent of TDs were built to North American specification.

twin leading shoes in the front drums, and the extra 4½in of width inside the body. Above all, the car was now available with left-hand drive – with, incidentally, both the main dials now always placed in front of the driver. In terms of styling, the TD was instantly recognisable as an MG Midget – a little lower and with a squatter stance, thanks to those fat tyres on the small disc wheels and the wider track, with wings that covered the wheels a little more fully, and with a slightly more daring rake to the spare wheel and fuel tank at the back. But the headlamps were still separate, the radiator was still a proper radiator, and the sweep of the wings and running boards still recalled the first swept-wing J2 of 1933.

It is fair to sum up the TD as a compromise, a car that carried forward the best traditions of its predecessors mixed with a sensible number of worthwhile modern features. It was a car that would still appeal to the old-school MG enthusiasts but which, because of its greater practicality, was also likely to bring new converts into the fold, especially in the USA, and often as not among women car buyers. The TD succeeded brilliantly – of the 29,664 production cars made from 1949 to 1953, no fewer than 23,488 or 79 per cent were built to North American export specification, while actual shipments to the USA numbered 20,007 cars.

The TD was warmly welcomed when it was launched in January 1950. Its home market price – including Purchase Tax – was £567 7s 3d, a not unreasonable increase on the TC's final price of £527 16s 8d and comparing well with the Morgan 4/4 Two-seater

at £556 11s 8d or the Singer Nine Roadster at £575 15s, while the cheapest HRG, the 1100, was just over £1000. The new model was soon put through its paces by the magazine road-testers, the same car being used by both *The Autocar* and *The Motor* in turn. The former recorded a top speed of 80-83mph, the latter an average of 77mph with a best one-way run of almost 83mph. *The Motor* got the best acceleration times, of 13.5secs to 50mph and 21.5secs to 60mph – *The Autocar*'s times were about 2secs worse in both cases – and fuel consumption figures of between 26 and 33mpg were quoted. Neither road test found anything major to criticise about the car, and if disappointment was felt over the fact that the TD had exactly the same power output as the TC, it was left unexpressed. The TD's performance was in fact all but identical to that of the TA some 15 years earlier, yet as a measure of how far things had progressed elsewhere in the meantime, there was in Britain in 1950 a 1.5-litre six-seater saloon which offered performance comparable to the TD – the Jowett Javelin.

The TD went through its four-year production life with only the barest of modifications. One of the important changes, the introduction of an 8in clutch instead of the original 7¼in size, occurred in July 1951, at which time the engine number prefix was changed from XPAG-TD to XPAG-TD2. In early 1952 a water temperature gauge was added to the instrumentation, and several changes were made in the autumn of that year, including the introduction of a foot-operated dip switch, an improved three-bow hood, a new design of round

External differences between a standard TD and the Mark II model are few, but the small bulge on the side of the bonnet, just above the sidelamp, is for a larger air manifold on Mark II cars. Compare the altered top line of the sidescreens with the picture on page 59.

The TD had a much-modified dashboard layout with both main dials in front of the driver, while there was a glovebox (often used for fitting a radio) in front of the passenger. On this 1952 model a water temperature gauge shares the dial with the oil pressure gauge.

rear lamps, the addition of flashing indicators on North American models and the wiper motor being moved to the centre of the windscreen frame. So equipped the TD continued into 1953.

Meanwhile there had been a couple of diversions on the way. A tuned sports version of the TD had seen the light as early as 1950, when such a car was prepared for Dick Jacobs to race, and small numbers of similar cars were constructed in the same year, but from 1951 onwards the 'TD Mark II' became a regular production option, mainly for the American market. Also known as the 'TDC' model from its chassis number prefix, where 'C' presumably stood for Competition, these cars had broadly speaking a Stage 1 machined cylinder head with larger valves, a raised compression ratio and larger carburettors, resulting in 57-61bhp depending on exact specification. A higher final drive ratio, additional friction shock absorbers, dual fuel pumps and a manual ignition control were other distinguishing features. From June 1952 the engine number prefix on the Mark II models was changed to XPAG-TD3, and at the end of 1952 special 'Mark II' enamel badges were fitted, together with chrome-plated instead of painted radiator slats, and, for the first time on an MG, a black-and-white radiator badge instead of brown-and-cream. On these later cars,

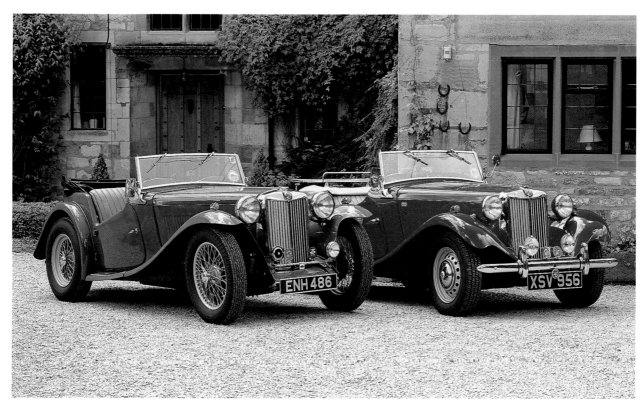

Comparison of a TA and TD. While the family resemblance is obvious and dimensions did not change greatly, the new car had a very different stance thanks to its smaller disc wheels. Bumpers had now become an essential requirement, not only in the American market.

TD under-bonnet views are interesting because this is a tuned TD Mark II (or TDC) model. The larger carburettors, air filter and air manifold, and also the dual fuel pumps, can be seen (above). The ignition side of the engine, on the other hand, is identical to the standard model (right).

A North American specification TF with optional wire wheels and luggage rack, the latter a useful Midget accessory that had been offered as early as 1933. *Road & Track* magazine judged the TF 'an anomaly – a retrogression'.

the compression ratio was standardised at 8.1:1, instead of the 7.25:1 of the ordinary TD. Total production of the Mark II specification cars was 1710, of which 1593 were built to North American specification.

Then there was the Arnolt-MG. This came from two Bertone-bodied TDs, a coupé and a convertible, shown in Turin in 1952. They were seen by S. H. 'Wacky' Arnolt, the Morris and MG distributor in Chicago, who immediately placed an order for 100 of each with Bertone. In fact only 100 were made altogether: 65 coupés and 35 convertibles (apart from the two original show cars). The coachwork was in the contemporary Italian style but incorporated the traditional MG radiator grille, and the cars were two-plus-two seaters with roomy boots. Arnolt arranged for TD chassis to be shipped directly from Abingdon to Turin where the bodies were hand-built in the Bertone factory and the finished cars sent to the USA. The Arnolt-MG at $3145 was about $1000 or 50 per cent more expensive than a standard TD, so not surprisingly it was not all that popular and Arnolt was still trying to sell the last ones in 1958, by which time he had gone on to the Arnolt-Bristol Bolide, a Bristol chassis again with a Bertone body. Around half of the Arnolt-MGs are known still to exist, now including a few examples which have come to the UK from the USA.

This was not the only special-bodied TD, either. Perhaps the best known of the rest was the long-wheelbase TD four-seater offered by the New York MG distributor, Inskip. This had the frame extended by 10in, noticeably wider doors and front bucket seats. About 12 of these cars were built, probably all as conversions from standard models. Production records reveal that a total of 166 TDs was supplied as chassis, mostly left-hand drive export versions, of which the Arnolt cars only account for about 100. It seems that quite a few TDs were bodied by small German or Swiss coachbuilders, such as Ghia-Aigle, for whom none other than Giovanni Michelotti did a TD design in 1952, but many were rather bulbous, heavy-looking cars. A Dutch coachbuilder, Veth of Arnhem, built a razor-edged semi-fastback coupé on a TD chassis, forming an interesting link between the P-type Airline and the MGB GT of the next decade.

Puzzling over how to replace the TD, Syd Enever came up with a prototype styled on the lines of George Phillips' 1951 Le Mans car but featuring a new perimeter-style chassis frame which permitted a much lower seating position. Unfortunately, by the time this car was ready in 1952 MG had a new master, Leonard Lord once again, now chairman of the new BMC combine. He initially turned the new car down and only changed his mind a year or so later, when he allowed MG to go ahead with the all-enveloping streamlined sports car which in due course made its appearance as the MGA in 1955. All that MG was allowed to do with the TD in 1952 was to give it a modest facelift, which was introduced as the TF at the London Motor Show in 1953 alongside a new MG saloon which revived the Magnette

Cutaway drawing from the TD sales brochure shows the new chassis that is swept over the rear axle, the independent front suspension and the disc wheels.

Wire wheels became available again on the TF, but they originally had a painted finish, not chromed.

PYT 658 is the TF from the Heritage Motor Centre collection at **Gaydon, here photographed in earlier years at Donington Park.**

name. Although some traditionalists were upset by the choice of Magnette for the new saloon it was still this car which grabbed the headlines and caught the public's fancy – it made the TF look very old hat indeed. Nobody at the time liked the TF very much. Celebrated American road tester 'Uncle' Tom McCahill, writing in *Mechanix Illustrated*, said that 'It went over like boils on an acrobat' and summed it up as 'Mrs Casey's dead cat, slightly warmed over'.

Later generations have found the TF more appealing. The styling modifications centred around the front end of the car, which had new front wings into which the headlamps were countersunk and a radiator grille which was well raked back – it was now truly a grille, for the filler cap on top was non-functional and the actual radiator filler was under the bonnet. The bonnet was lowered at the front and the bonnet side panels were fixed. The basic body tub was very much like the TD's but the fuel tank and spare wheel were angled further forward and the rear wings were extended backwards.

The interior was comprehensively updated, with new individual seats and an all-new dashboard featuring three centrally-mounted dials in octagonal bezels. The most important mechanical alteration was that the TF engine, now designated type XPAG-TF, had the higher compression ratio and thus the 57bhp of the later TD Mark II. Wire wheels were now offered as an alternative to the TD-style disc wheels. In the UK the new model cost £780 5s 10d including Purchase Tax when introduced, an increase of £20 in the basic price over the TD, and a price which frankly compared unfavourably with the £787 7s 6d charged for the new Triumph TR2. The Triumph was an up-to-date looking 2-litre car with a top speed of 100mph and decent luggage accommodation – in comparison the MG was old-fashioned, slow and inconvenient.

No road test of the TF was ever published in Britain. In the USA, *Road & Track*, while not trying to rival Tom McCahill's colourful language, described the TF as 'an anomaly – a retrogression', but still summed it up as 'America's Best Sports Car Buy' at $2260 plus $135 for the optional wire wheels. They recorded a top speed of 80mph. At Abingdon the factory was only too aware of the generation gap that had opened up between the TF

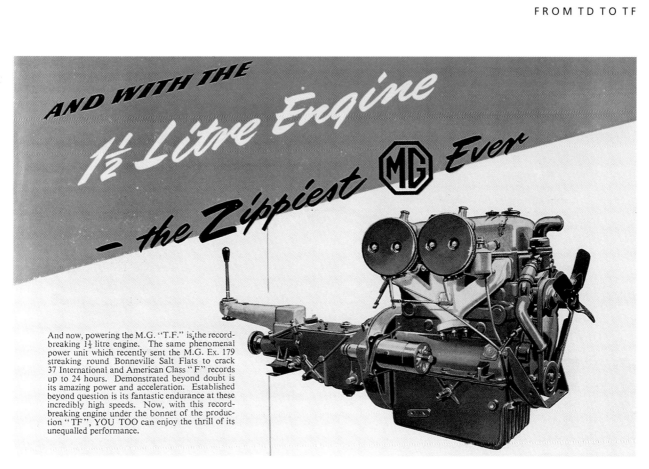

AND WITH THE 1½ Litre Engine — the Zippiest MG Ever

And now, powering the M.G. "T.F." is the record-breaking 1½ litre engine. The same phenomenal power unit which recently sent the M.G. Ex. 179 streaking round Bonneville Salt Flats to crack 37 International and American Class "F" records up to 24 hours. Demonstrated beyond doubt is its amazing power and acceleration. Established beyond question is its fantastic endurance at these incredibly high speeds. Now, with this record-breaking engine under the bonnet of the production "TF", YOU TOO can enjoy the thrill of its unequalled performance.

'The Zippiest MG ever', the TF 1500 model, was mostly aimed at the American public. Power increased to 63bhp from the 1250 TF's 57bhp.

and newer cars such as the TR2 and the Austin-Healey 100. To satisfy the requirements of the US market John Thornley wanted two things: an aerodynamic all-enveloping body and a full 1.5-litre engine. After the TF had been in production for one year Morris Engines succeeded in enlarging the TF's engine to 1466cc, fulfilling at least one of Thornley's wishes. This was done by siamesing the cylinders in two pairs, thus permitting an increase in the bore to 72mm, and with a compression ratio of 8.3:1 the revised XPEG-type engine gave 63bhp. Other than the engine – which looked just the same – there were only small 'TF 1500' badges on either side of the bonnet and small rear reflectors to distinguish the new model which, being mainly aimed at the North American market, had a very low-key introduction.

We are again indebted to *Road & Track*, who carried out a road test of the TF 1500, measuring a top speed of 85mph, while the 0-60mph acceleration time had been improved from the 18.9secs of the 1250 model to 16.3secs. Gas mileage was also a little better, at 23-26 mpg (US gallons, of course) from the 20-23mpg of the 1250 model. Not the least significant factor was that the American list price had now been reduced to $1995. The TF 1500 was 'now more than ever a fun-car [and] even better value'.

The 1500 model went quietly into production in July 1954 but was at first built almost exclusively for export to the USA. For a few months the 1250 and 1500 models were built side by side, and when the last 1250 model came off the line in September 1954 the production figure for this model had reached exactly 6200. The 1500 then continued alone until April 1955, only 3400 of this type being made, of which a mere 244 cars were home market models as against 813 TF 1250s. In mid-1954, when the new MGA project had been given BMC's official blessing, Abingdon had begun to gear up for this model, which went into production in May 1955. So for a time the Midget line came to an end: the TF 1250 had been the last T-series car to be described as a Midget, the 1500 version being called simply the TF 1500. With their combined production of 52,646 cars the T-series far outnumbered the overhead camshaft models which between 1928 and 1936 only reached a combined total of 8541 cars. In their turn the T-series would be

A TF in its element, a winding English country road, with owner Tony Newbold at the wheel (left). Engine accessibility on the TF was somewhat compromised as only the top panels of the bonnet opened, the sides being fixed (below). As the bonnet line was lower than on the TD, small individual air cleaners were fitted. The interior (below left) was all new on the TF, with separate seats and a new dashboard design featuring a central instrument panel with three dials in octagonal bezels.

This brochure was clearly intended for the US market, where two-thirds of TFs were sold.

Built on the TD chassis, this is the Bertone-built coupé sold by S.H. Arnolt, Nuffield's distributor in Chicago – a convertible version was also available.

overshadowed by the MGA, the modern Midget from 1961 onwards, and the MGB.

The original line of MG Midgets endured for some 25 years. Although not quite the first affordable small sports car and never completely without rivals in the market, it was nevertheless MG which became synonymous with this particular type of car. Without the MG Midget Britain would most likely never have developed the tradition for small, popular sports cars – a tradition which, despite the hiatus from 1981 to 1995,

has been kept alive in the minds and hearts of enthusiasts. Without the MG Midget, America would never have started its equally long love affair with sports cars, nor would the Japanese motor industry have produced modern reincarnations such as the Mazda MX5 Miata. There is no greater tribute imaginable to Cecil Kimber's original inspiration. Even if the modern MGF is no longer called a 'Midget' – and indeed its engine size puts it outside the Midget class – the spirit of its predecessors lives on.

T SERIES IN COMPETITION

The TA was not particularly suitable for competition work. Its worst handicap was the long-stroke engine, which was not particularly responsive to tuning. Nevertheless, the successes of the factory-sponsored trials teams in 1936, coupled with the fact that these teams were now running models no longer in production, prompted MG to build new trials cars based on the TA for both the Cream Cracker and the Musketeer teams for 1937. These original trials TAs were little modified mechanically but the flowing wings of the standard production cars were replaced by skimpy cycle-type wings, looking particularly effective on the Cream Cracker cars in the paint scheme of cream with brown wings, while the Musketeer cars were painted all red. Knobbly off-road tyres were fitted and two spare wheels were carried. At the end of the 1937 season the Cream Crackers again carried off the MCC Team Championship Trophy.

More extensively modified cars were built for 1938, the Musketeer cars being fitted with superchargers and the Cream Cracker cars getting 1548cc engines from the new MG VA – a simple enough thing to do as the VA engine was basically only a big-bore TA unit. When this did not prove totally satisfactory the cars instead received 1707cc engines which had been bored out to 73mm, the dimension of the six-cylinder WA model. Such engines were also fitted in small numbers of VAs, typically tourers supplied for Police use, and were RAC rated at 14hp. These modified cars enabled the Cream Crackers to win the championship trophy for a third time. The 1937 Cream Cracker cars were taken over by a Scottish team known as the Highlanders and were painted dark blue. The Cream Crackers team was disbanded in early 1939 but the Musketeers and the Highlanders continued to compete in trials until the outbreak of the war.

The 1250cc XPAG engine of the TB and the post-war TC models was much more robust and able to withstand far more tuning work. Not surprising, therefore, that when motor sport was resumed in the late 1940s MGs quickly became favourites for less well-off amateur sportsmen – not only in Britain but in many

One of the special TA trials cars. BBL 83 was J.A.Bastock's car from the 'Musketeers' team in 1938, fitted with a Marshall supercharger, skimpy cycle-type wings and 16in wheels with knobbly tyres. Here it is on the Barnstaple Trial.

European countries as well as Australia and North America. Demand from private owners led MG in 1949 to issue the first tuning booklet, describing in detail five stages of tuning for the XPAG engine, including the fitting of a supercharger. Although MG sold a wide range of tuning parts, the company was anxious to stress that super-tuning would invalidate the guarantee, that they would not supply new cars in tuned form or tune customers' cars, and that, above all else, 'Power Costs Money'!

Such stern warnings did little to deter the new generation of MG enthusiasts. In the USA, MGs had already been raced before the war by a small but enthusiastic band of amateurs, led by the Collier brothers

George Phillips, who became the photographer for *Autosport*, **the new British motor sporting magazine launched in** 1950, **ran two MG-based specials at Le Mans. The streamlined body of the TD-based special he used in 1951 inspired the shape of the MGA.**

TDs racing in 1950. Dick Jacobs pushes hard (top) on his way to second place in Silverstone's production sports car race. The TDs of George Philips (50) and Ted Lund (48) sandwich an HRG in the Ulster TT (above), held at Dundrod.

(the original MG importers in New York) who helped to found the Automobile Racing Club of America. Some of the more notable events contested by MGs in America in the late 1930s were the Alexandria Bay Round the Houses races, the Climb to the Clouds hillclimb at Mount Washington in New Hampshire, and the race meetings at the Roosevelt Raceway on Long Island. The ARCA was disbanded in 1941 but in 1944 the Sports Car Club of America was formed, and an MG-owning SCCA member, Cameron Argetsinger, conceived and organised the first Watkins Glen Grand Prix in upstate New York, held in 1948. Not a Grand Prix in the European sense, the Watkins Glen race was a road race for sports cars, typically with various individual races for cars of different

size, and despite increasing competition in the small capacity class, MGs continued to hold their own through the years until 1955.

MGs also contested many other of the early sports car races in the USA, including Bridgehampton on Long Island, Elkhart Lake in Wisconsin, Pebble Beach in California (now the scene of the world's most exclusive classic car concours event) and, most famously, Sebring in Florida, where the series of endurance races started on New Year's Eve 1950. MGs did well in their class in the early Sebring races. Some American drivers adopted the English Lester-MG instead of the standard cars and others built their own specials, including Gus Ehrman, whose Motto looked like a miniature Ferrari, and expatriate Englishman Ken Miles with his MGR1 and the incredibly low-slung MGR2.

In England there were also several different MG-based specials. One of the most famous was the special-bodied TC which George Phillips ran at Le Mans in 1949, doing quite well until the car was disqualified because of a misunderstanding between Phillips' co-driver and their mechanic. Undeterred, and with a new co-driver, Phillips returned to Le Mans in 1950 and was rewarded with a second place (behind a Jowett Jupiter) in the 1500cc class. MG was suitably impressed with Phillips' efforts as a privateer and offered to build a special car for him for the 1951 race. This was based on a TD chassis which Syd Enever fitted with a full-width streamlined body, and was known by its experimental number EX172 or by its registration mark UMG 400.

THE
NEW
MG
MIDGET
SERIES "TD"
MARK II

N A NUFFIELD PRODUCT

● HIGH PERFORMANCE ● FIRM SUSPENSION ● PRECISION STEERING ● SUPERLATIVE BRAKES

Seen on the cover of the TD Mark II brochure, FMO 885 was one of the 1950 works racing cars, used by Dick Jacobs, and was unique in being fitted with bucket seats.

Goldie Gardner at Utah with EX135, his famous record-breaker. Although this car was based on a K3 Magnette chassis, by 1952 when the picture was taken the car was fitted with a developed version of the TD's XPAG engine.

While sadly the car was soon out of the 1951 Le Mans race – a valve broke, knocking a hole in the piston – the shape of the car served as the inspiration for the later MGA production car. Unfortunately neither of the Phillips Le Mans MGs exists today.

Phillips, together with Dick Jacobs and Ted Lund, had become an 'unofficial official' MG works driver. The trio had works-prepared TCs for some 1949 races, and in 1950 they were given TDs with tuned engines – in effect the first of the TD Mark II models. In the *Daily Express* production car race at Silverstone in August 1950 the trio came second, third and fourth in the 1500cc class (which was won by an HRG), while in the following month, in the first post-war TT race held at Dundrod near Belfast, the three MGs came first, second and third in class, with Jacobs in the leading car finishing 16th overall. The works-prepared TDs continued to race in 1951, Jacobs winning the 1500cc class in the production car race at

Silverstone, but as competition increased these fairly standard cars with 1250cc engines were at a disadvantage in their class as they were running against full 1.5-litre cars, not only the HRGs and the new Jowett Jupiters but also MG-derived cars such as the Lester-MG and the Cooper-MG, while overbored 1500cc TD engines were also used in cars built by Kieft, Lister and Lotus.

These were the twilight years for MG in competition, with only sporadic works support for private drivers, but things eventually took a turn for the better when in 1954 it was decided that BMC should set up a formal competitions department headed by Marcus Chambers. It took a while for the new organisation to find its feet in motor sport for there were many teething troubles to overcome, not least the difficulty at first of finding suitable cars to enter in various events. In the first year of full activity, 1955, a variety of BMC cars were tried out in different rallies and races including the RAC Rally,

This early Cooper driven by Cliff Davis (above), with looks reminiscent of a contemporary Ferrari, was one of several British specialist sports cars which used MG engines in the early 1950s. Pat Moss (left) finished third in the Ladies' Cup with a works TF 1500 on the 1955 RAC Rally.

where an MG TF 1500 was entered for Pat Moss and Pat Faichney, who came third in the Ladies' Cup. Three TF 1500s were run in the Circuit of Ireland, where seasoned rally drivers Ian and Pat Appleyard came fourth overall, while a class win and the team prize were gained in the Scottish Rally in June 1955 – the TF's swansong because in the same month the MGA prototypes appeared in the Le Mans 24 Hours.

In terms of record breaking the Gardner-MG, also known as EX135, which had originally been built in 1938 based on a K3 Magnette, was brought out again after the war and continued to break records in different classes, fitted with a variety of engines. In 1951 the car was fitted with a supercharged TD engine and taken to the Bonneville salt flats in Utah where it set six long-distance records in the 1500cc class at speeds up to 137.4mph. A further attempt followed in 1952 when officially measured speeds were up to 189.5mph and two

further records were set, but this was to some extent a disappointing result, as the car had been unofficially timed at well over 200mph. However, this was to be the last outing for the car and its driver.

George Eyston now approached Leonard Lord of BMC with the suggestion that MG should build a new record car for him to drive. Syd Enever had by this time completed the new chassis design for EX175, which ultimately became the MGA, and there was a spare chassis frame available. This was fitted with one of the new XPEG engines of 1466cc and a streamlined body based on the design of EX135. It was decided to run this car in unsupercharged form, and in its original form the car had left-hand drive. EX179 was taken out to Utah in 1954 and George Eyston and Ken Miles duly took eight records at speeds up to almost 154mph, including the 12-hour record at just over 120mph. EX179 continued its record-breaking career in subsequent years and was fitted with different engines, first of the MGA Twin Cam type, later with an Austin-Healey Sprite engine. In the same way that EX135 is preserved today with the XPAG engine of 1952, so EX179 is still fitted with the Sprite engine which was used at the end of its active career in 1959. Both cars are part of the BMIHT collection in the Heritage Motor Centre at Gaydon.

MIDGET LEGACY

When this book was first published the youngest of the cars described in it was marking its 40th birthday – yet they continue to generate an amazing enthusiasm, even in a generation that was not yet born when the last TF came off the Abingdon assembly line. MGs, of almost any model, have long since been accepted as classic cars – they were collected, cherished and restored even before the classic car movement was properly started. In Britain the MG Car Club, founded in 1930, is one of the oldest one-make car clubs with a continuous history, supplemented in later years by the MG Owners' Club and also by the Octagon Car Club, which is concerned only with pre-1956 models. In the USA the New England MG T Register was founded in 1964, again catering for the pre-1956 cars, and there are numerous other MG clubs in many of those countries where MGs were traditionally exported, including most parts of Europe, South Africa, Canada, Australia, New Zealand and Japan. When *Classic Cars* magazine was launched in Britain in 1973 the first issue

Old MGs neither die nor fade away – they keep on racing. A wet day at

Oulton Park in 1979 for assorted T-types in an MG Car Club race.

had an MG TC on its cover (together with the then new MGB GT V8). In both Britain and in the USA there are now specialised independent magazines which deal only with MGs. There are numerous events for MG cars: static rallies, road runs and even special race series, usually organised by the various clubs, while the availability of spare parts for many of the older MGs, especially the T-series cars, is remarkable.

All this has become possible because of the comparatively large numbers of these cars originally made and because their survival rate measured against their contemporaries is quite simply staggering. For instance, of the 2500 P-types it seems likely that almost 1000 survive – and of the pre-war racing models almost every single car survives or is at least fully accounted for. In the modern age old cars frequently make journeys half way round the globe – many cars originally sold in the USA are being bought by European, Australian or Japanese collectors. It is likely that since the height of the classic car boom in the late 1980s the number of T-series cars in Britain has seen a substantial net increase, with more cars coming in from North America than are sold to Europe or Japan. Yet the MG movement in North America continues to thrive despite the numbers of cars sold out of the USA and Canada.

It would now be extremely unusual to find a pre-1956 MG which had not at some stage in its long life been refurbished or restored. Not surprisingly, many cars have been lovingly restored to almost better than original condition, but others live surprisingly hard lives – even in 1994, pre-1934 MGs were setting new national long-distance class records in the hands of MG Car Club members, and many others were being campaigned in historic racing. Equally arduous were the long-distance driving events undertaken by the American enthusiasts of the New England MG T Register, who have for instance driven T-types across the USA and to Alaska.

Owning an overhead camshaft model is the greater challenge. These cars were always slightly more temperamental and susceptible to malfunction after the ministrations of cack-handed mechanics. Not a few of these cars suffered the indignity of having their original engine units replaced with, for instance, sidevalve Ford, Morris Eight or Morris Ten engines or, most legitimately, overhead camshaft Morris Minor engines. Others had their mechanical braking systems converted to hydraulics, or had decrepit coachwork replaced by home-made special bodies – which may have seemed like a good idea at the time but was rarely an improvement on the original! Parts availability for the overhead camshaft cars is actually quite good, with a small number of dedicated specialists active in this field.

T-series cars are more easy to deal with for the restorer, and easier also to keep on the road. However, more than a few TAs have over the years had their original engines replaced with the later and better XPAG engines from TBs or from post-war models – original MPJG engines are now a rather scarce commodity. In general terms, as long as there is a basic chassis frame and an engine for a T-type, almost anything else can be rebuilt or replaced. A new body, whether of the standard two-seater type or even of the TA/TB Tickford drophead coupé type, can be supplied ready-made or built to special order. Complete trim kits are likewise available, and most other parts are available in remanufactured or refurbished form.

None of these cars will present a great challenge to the enthusiast in terms of keeping the car running, assuming a limited annual mileage. The overhead camshaft cars will need a bit more in the way of servicing and maintenance. Their mechanical brakes and unsynchronised gearboxes demand slightly greater driving skills but they are fundamentally as good natured as MGs normally are, and are easily mastered with a little practice. The only serious drawback of these cars is that they are frankly cramped for drivers over average size. The T-series are much more comfortable, especially the TD and TF with their wider bodies, but even these models have narrow footwells with pedals set close together.

The sports car character of these MGs is indicated not so much by their performance, which by modern standards is definitely on the modest side, as by their behaviour. The steering, whether of the early worm-and-wheel type, the Bishop Cam type or the rack-and-pinion of the TD/TF, is light and precise, and very high geared: 1½ turns from lock to lock on the early T-types and even on the TD/TF less than 3 turns. The ride is firm, especially on the models with semi-elliptic springs all round, but still far from compliant on the models with independent front suspension. The gearchange on the original M-type with its three-speed 'box and long gear lever took a little getting to know, but on subsequent models with remote control change and four-speed 'box the short, precise movements of the gear lever made changing a pleasure. These are compact cars, with a

The Naylor TF 1700 was a modernised replica built by long-time T-series restorer Alastair Naylor. Here the first three cars off the production line **are presented to their new owners – Mr and Mrs C.Rycroft bought two cars in white! Just over 100 Naylor TFs were built before the venture failed.**

This may look like a C-type racing Midget, but it is a replica built on a D-type chassis and fitted with a J-type engine. Such specials are completely legitimate as long as they are not passed off as the real thing. If in doubt try to verify such cars with MG Car Club experts.

wheel at each corner, and it is easy for the driver to judge the exact position of the car and place it accordingly on the road. Like all true thoroughbreds they respond best when they are handled correctly, but they are also quite tolerant and forgiving. With the exception of the hairy racing models of the 1930s – which are unlikely to be used much on the road anyway – there is not a Midget or T-series MG which in original unmodified form is too fast for the abilities of its chassis.

Which then is the best of the bunch? A difficult question to answer as so much comes down to personal preference. It is both easier and less controversial to suggest that the later cars, the TD and TF models, are probably the most practical. Of the overhead camshaft cars the last variation, the PB, is likely to be regarded as the most desirable version, with its slightly more powerful and more robust engine. But each and every model has its protagonists. The most sought-after and therefore most valuable cars are the racing models, which change hands very infrequently, but any proven competition history of an individual car would be likely to make it more interesting. Some of the special-bodied cars would also command a premium, depending on their provenance and how attractive they are, although inevitably they are far more difficult to restore.

Given the long-standing popularity of the classic MGs it is not surprising that over the years there have been several attempts at recreating them. Perhaps these imitations really began with the Morgan in the 1930s – although this make became a success in its own right and has, despite the odds, managed to survive as a builder of traditional-looking sports cars. Another contemporary imitator was the Italian Siata company, which in the early 1950s offered a TD lookalike based on Fiat 1400 running gear. When the original T-series cars became sought-after

classics, several latter-day imitators appeared. In Britain in the 1970s there were several kit cars which aped the traditional MG style but which were usually based on Triumph Herald chassis! The Spartan was one of the better-known attempts but more successful as a TF imitator was the Gentry with its TF-style wheels, bumpers and even an MG grille – although usually borrowed from the Z-type Magnette saloon.

Designed to fool the unwary was the Lafer MP which hailed from the unlikely source of Brazil – from a distance the illusion of a TD was almost perfect but the carefully contoured mock fuel tank and spare wheel opened to reveal a VW Beetle engine, as the MP was based on a Volkswagen chassis. Launched in 1974, it enjoyed quite a vogue and was exported to several European countries.

Far more respectable was the Naylor TF 1700, the brainchild of long-standing and highly respected T-type restorer Alastair Naylor in Yorkshire. This was an intelligently and sensibly modernised TF, faithful to the original in many ways but for instance with built-in flashing indicators discreetly mounted in the bumpers and front-hinged doors. The running gear was also modern, using the 1700cc O-series engine from 1980s Austin Rover models. It was a fully-fledged production car and the only MG replica to be given the unreserved blessing of BL. It met with an enthusiastic reception when it was launched in 1985. Aimed squarely at the 'nostalgia' market, it was quite the best of several 1980s efforts at recreating classic British sports cars, but never quite sold in large enough numbers to be completely viable. Alastair Naylor eventually decided to return to his original field as a leading parts supplier and restorer, and his car passed into other hands, being rebadged as the Hutson, before eventually going out of production altogether.

APPENDIX

Identification & production ....

M-type
Production period, Mar 1929 to Jun 1932. Chassis numbers prefixed M. Chassis numbers from M.0251 to M.3485. Total production, 3235 cars (fabric-bodied two-seaters, 2329; metal-panelled two-seaters, 273; fabric-bodied coupés, 493; metal-panelled coupés, 37; Double-Twelve race cars and replicas, 21; chassis, 82).

C-type
Production period, Mar 1931 to Jun 1932. Chassis numbers prefixed C. Chassis numbers from C.0251 to C.0294. Total production, 44 cars.

D-type
Production period, Oct 1931 to May 1932. Chassis numbers prefixed D. Chassis numbers from D.0251 to D.500. Total production, 250 cars (four-seaters, 208; salonettes, 37; chassis, 5).

J-types
Production period: J1, Jul 1932 to Jul 1933; J2, Jul 1932 to Jan 1934; J3, Nov 1932 to Sep 1933; J4, Mar to Jul 1933. Chassis numbers prefixed J. Chassis numbers: J1, J.0252 to J.0632; J2, J.0251, J.2001 to J.3750, J.4101 to J.4432; J3, J.3751 to J.3772; J4, J.4001 to J.4009. Total production: J1, 381 cars (four-seaters, 262; salonettes, 117; converted to J2 two-seaters, 2); J2, 2083 cars (two-seaters, 2061, of which approximately 600 were swept-wing 1934 models; chassis, 22); J3, 22 cars; J4, 9 cars.

P-types
Production period: P (PA), Jan 1934 to Jul 1935; PB, Jul 1935 to Feb 1936. Chassis numbers prefixed P or PB. Chassis numbers: P (PA), P.0251 to P.2250. PB, PB.0251 to PB.0775. Total production: P (PA), 2000 cars (two-seaters, 1394; four-seaters, 498; Airline coupés, 28; chassis 53; converted to PBs, 27); PB, 525 cars (two-seaters, 408; four-seaters, 99; Airline coupés, 14; chassis, 4).

Q-type
Production period, May to Sep 1934. Chassis numbers prefixed QA. Chassis numbers from QA.0251 to QA.0258. Total production, 8 cars.

R-type
Production period, Apr 1935 only. Chassis numbers prefixed RA. Chassis numbers from RA.0251 to RA.0260. Total production, 10 cars.

(Note: Production figures for ohc models are based on figures compiled by Mike Allison of the MG Car Club's Triple-M Register.)

TA-series
Production period, Mar 1936 to Apr 1939. Chassis numbers prefixed TA. Chassis numbers from TA.0251 to TA.3253. Total production, 3003 cars (two-seaters, 2722; Tickford drophead coupés, 260; Airline coupés, 2; unassembled for export, 8; chassis, 11, of which 10 for export to Australia).

TB-series
Production period, Apr to Oct 1939. Chassis numbers prefixed TB. Chassis numbers from TB.0251 to TB.0629. Total production, 379 cars (two-seaters, 319; Tickford drophead coupés, 60).

TC-series
Production period, Sep 1945 to Nov 1949. Chassis numbers prefixed TC. Chassis numbers from TC.0252 to TC.10251 (TC.0251 was a prototype). Total production, 10000 cars (home market, 3408; RHD export, 4497; North American export, 2001, of which at least 494 to EX-U specification; CKD cars for Eire, 84; chassis, 10).

TD-series
Production period, Nov 1949 to Aug 1953. Chassis numbers prefixed TD (TD-C on TD Mark II models). Chassis numbers from TD.0252 to TD.29915 (TD.0251 was a prototype). Total production, 29664 cars (home market, 1656; RHD export, 2955; LHD export, 956; LHD North American export, 23488; RHD chassis, 9; LHD chassis, 157; RHD CKD cars for Eire and South Africa, 443). These figures include 1710 Mark II models (home market, 51; RHD export, 51; LHD export, 13; LHD North American export, 1593; LHD chassis, 2).

TF-series
Production period, Sep 1953 to Apr 1955. Chassis numbers prefixed with five-character code starting 'HD' (on maker's guarantee plate), with TF where stamped on chassis. Chassis numbers: TF with 1250cc engine, 501 to 6500, 6651 to 6750, 6851 to 6950; TF 1500, 6501 to 6650, 6751 to 6850, 6951 to 10100 (TF.0250 and TF.0251 were prototypes). Total production, 6200 TFs and 3400 TF 1500s (home market 813 TFs and 244 TF 1500s; RHD export, 1207 TFs and 522 TF 1500s; LHD export, 420 TFs and 72 TF 1500s; LHD North American export, 3746 TFs and 2487 TF 1500s; RHD North American export, 2 TFs; RHD chassis, 2 TFs, for home market; RHD CKD cars for Eire, 10 TFs; LHD CKD cars for Mexico, 75 TF 1500s).

Technical specifications ....

M-type
Engine In-line four-cylinder **Construction** Cast-iron block and head **Crankshaft** Two main bearings **Bore × stroke** 57mm × 83mm (2.244in × 3.268in) **Capacity** 847cc (51.7cu in) **Valves** Single overhead camshaft, shaft driven **Compression ratio** 5.4:1 (12/12 race cars 6.4:1, 12/12 replicas 6.0:1) **Fuel system** One horizontal SU 1⅛in carburettor (12/12 race cars, single Solex) **Maximum power** 20bhp at 4000rpm (12/12 cars and all cars from engine number 2024, 27bhp at 4500rpm) **Transmission** Three-speed Wolseley-type manual gearbox, four-speed 'box optional on later cars **Final drive ratio** 4.89:1 **Top gear mph per 1000rpm** 16.9mph **Brakes** Mechanical, 8in drums front and rear, on early cars with rod operation and transmission handbrake, later cars cable operation and handbrake on all four wheels **Front suspension** Beam axle, semi-elliptic leaf springs, friction shock absorbers **Rear suspension** Live axle, semi-elliptic leaf springs, friction shock absorbers **Steering** Adamant worm and wheel **Wheels/tyres**

Bolt-on 19 × 2½ wire wheels, 4.00-19 tyres **Length** 123in (3124mm) **Wheelbase** 78in (1981mm) **Width** 50in (1270mm) **Height** 54in (1372mm) **Front track** 42in (1067mm) **Rear track** 42in (1067mm) **Unladen weight** Fabric-bodied two-seater 1134 lb (515kg), panelled two-seater 1281lb (582kg), fabric-bodied coupé 1302lb (591kg), panelled coupé 1386lb (629kg) **Top speed** 65mph (105kph) **0-40mph** 12sec **Typical fuel consumption** 36-40mpg

D-type
As M-type except: **Maximum power** All cars 27bhp at 4500rpm **Transmission** Remote control gearchange **Final drive ratio** 5.375:1 **Top gear mph per 1000rpm** 14.7mph **Brakes** Cable-operated on all cars **Wheels/tyres** Centrelock wire wheels **Length** 132in (3353mm) **Wheelbase** First 100 cars, 84in (2134mm); later cars, 86in (2184mm) **Unladen weight** Four-seater 1484lb (674kg), salonette 1638lb (744kg) **Top speed** Estimated 55-60mph (88-97kph)

C-type
As M-type except: **Bore × stroke** 57mm × 73mm (2.244in × 2.874in) **Capacity** 746cc (45.5cu in) **Compression ratio** Unsupercharged, 8.5:1; unsupercharged with cross-flow head, 9.0:1; supercharged with either head, 5.8:1 **Fuel system** One SU 1¼in carburettor; two carburettors on unsupercharged model with cross-flow head; supercharger if fitted: Powerplus no.7, 12psi boost **Maximum power** Standard model 37.4bhp at 6000rpm; with cross-flow head, 44.1bhp at 6400rpm; supercharged model, 44.9bhp at 6200rpm; supercharged model with cross-flow head, 52.5bhp at 6500rpm **Transmission** Four-speed ENV manual gearbox **Final drive ratio** 5.5:1 or 5.375:1 **Top gear mph per 1000rpm** 14.6mph or 14.7mph **Brakes** 12in drums on later cars, cable operation on all cars **Wheels/tyres** Centre-lock wire wheels **Length** 138in (3505mm) **Wheelbase** 81in (2057mm) **Width** 52in (1321mm) **Height** 49in (1245mm) **Unladen weight** 1134lb (515kg); also quoted as 1456lb (661kg) **Top speed** 88mph (141kph) **0-60mph** 20.8sec **Standing ¼-mile** 19.8sec **Typical fuel consumption** 27-30mpg (NB: Performance data for supercharged model tested by *The Autocar*, 10 November 1931, and *The Motor*, 3 December 1931)

J2 two-seater
Engine In-line four-cylinder **Construction** Cast-iron block and head **Crankshaft** Two main bearings **Bore × stroke** 57mm × 83mm (2.244in × 3.268in) **Capacity** 847cc (51.7cu in) **Valves** Single overhead camshaft, shaft driven **Compression ratio** Early cars 5.4:1, later 6.2:1; with tuned engine 6.7:1 **Fuel system** Two SU horizontal 1in carburettors; semi-downdraught from engine number 551 **Maximum power** Early cars 30.4bhp (with 5.4:1 CR); later 36bhp at 5500rpm (with 6.2:1 CR); tuned engines 43.9bhp with 6.7:1 CR) **Transmission** Four-speed Wolseley-type manual gearbox with remote control **Final drive ratio** 5.375:1 **Top gear mph per 1000rpm** 14.7mph **Brakes** Mechanical, 8in drums, cable operation **Front suspension** Beam axle, semi-elliptic leaf springs, friction shock absorbers **Rear suspension** Live axle, semi-elliptic leaf springs, friction shock absorbers **Steering** Marles Weller worm and peg **Wheels/tyres** Centre-lock 19 × 2½ wire wheels, 4.00-19 tyres **Length** 124in (3150mm) **Wheelbase** 86in (2184mm) **Width** 51.5in (1308mm) **Height** 52.5in (1334mm) **Front track** 42in (1067mm) **Rear track** 42in (1067mm) **Unladen weight** 1431lb (650kg) with cycle-type wings; 1934 swept-wing model from chassis no 3438, 1463lb (664kg) **Top speed** 75-80mph (121-129kph) **Typical fuel consumption** 35mpg

J1 four-seater
As J2 except: **Length** Four-seater tourer 130in (3302mm), salonette 124.5in (3162mm) **Height** Four-seater tourer 54.5in (1384mm), salonette 55in (1397mm) **Unladen weight** Four-seater tourer 1501lb (681kg), salonette 1631lb (740kg)

J3
As J2 except: **Bore × stroke** 57mm × 73mm (2.244in × 2.874in) **Capacity** 746cc (45.5cu in) **Compression ratio** 5.2:1 **Fuel system** One SU horizontal 1¼in carburettor; supercharger: Powerplus no.6A, 8-10psi boost, or no.7, 12psi boost **Maximum power** Estimated 70bhp at 6000rpm **Final drive ratio** 4.78:1 **Top gear mph per 1000rpm** 16.4mph **Unladen weight** 1481lb (672kg) **Top speed** Estimated 106mph (171kph)

J4
As J3 except: **Compression ratio** 5.5:1 Fuel system 1⅝in carburettor; supercharger; Powerplus no.7, 12psi boost, or no.8, 14psi boost **Maximum power** 72.3bhp at 6000rpm **Transmission** ENV gearbox **Final drive ratio** 5.375:1 **Top gear mph per 1000rpm** 15.2mph **Brakes** 12in drums **Steering** Bishop Cam worm and peg **Wheels/tyres** 4.50-19 tyres (NB: An unsupercharged version of the J4 was catalogued as the 'J5' but it is certain that no such car was ever built).

PA
Engine In-line four-cylinder **Construction** Cast-iron block and head **Crankshaft** Three main bearings **Bore × stroke** 57mm × 83mm (2.244in × 3.268in) **Capacity** 847cc (51.7cu in) **Valves** Single overhead camshaft, shaft driven **Compression ratio** 6.2:1 or 6.8:1 **Fuel system** Two SU semi-downdraught 1in carburettors **Maximum power** 34.9bhp at 5000rpm or 39.2bhp at 5700rpm **Transmission** Four-speed Wolseley-type manual gearbox with remote control **Final drive ratio** Standard 5.375:1, optional 5.875:1 or 5.125:1 **Top gear mph per 1000rpm** 14.7mph **Brakes** Mechanical, 12in drums, cable-operated **Front suspension** Beam axle, semi-elliptic leaf springs, friction shock absorbers **Rear suspension** Live axle, semi-elliptic leaf springs, Luvax hydraulic lever-arm shock absorbers **Steering** Worm and peg type, Marles Weller on early cars, Bishop Cam from chassis no.1287 **Wheels/tyres** Centre-lock 19 × 2½ wire wheels, 4.00-19 tyres **Length** Two-seater 131in (3327mm), four-seater 138in (3505mm) **Wheelbase** 87⁵⁄₁₆in (2218mm) **Width** 52.5in (1334mm) **Height** 51.5in (1308mm) **Front track** 42in (1067mm) **Rear track** 42in (1067mm) **Unladen weight** Two-seater 1659lb (753kg), four-seater 1722lb (782kg), Airline coupé 1764lb (801kg) **Top speed** 75mph (121kph) **0-60mph** 23sec **Standing ¼-mile** 23sec **Typical fuel consumption** 33-35mpg

PB
As PA except: **Bore × stroke** 60mm × 83mm (2.362in × 3.268in) **Capacity** 939cc (57.3cu in) **Compression ratio** 6.8:1 **Maximum power** 39.9bhp at 5500rpm, later cars 43.5bhp at 5500rpm **Steering** Bishop Cam on all cars **Unladen weight** Four-seater 1729lb (785kg); two-seater and coupé, as for PA

Q-type
Engine In-line four-cylinder **Construction** Cast-iron block and head **Crankshaft** Three main bearings **Bore × stroke** 57mm × 73mm (2.244in × 2.874in) **Capacity** 746cc (45.5cu in) **Valves** Single overhead camshaft, shaft driven **Compression ratio** 6.4:1 **Fuel system** One SU 1⅞in horizontal carburettor; supercharger; Zoller no.4, 28psi boost **Maximum power** 113bhp at 7200rpm **Transmission** Four-speed ENV Wilson pre-selector gearbox **Final drive ratio** 4.125:1, 4.5:1 or 4.875:1 **Top gear mph per 1000rpm** 18.5mph **Brakes** Mechanical, 12in drums, cable-operated **Front suspension** Beam axle, semi-elliptic springs, friction shock absorbers **Rear suspension** Live axle, semi-elliptic springs, Luvax hydraulic lever-arm shock absorbers **Steering** Bishop Cam worm and peg type **Wheels/tyres** Centre-lock 18 × 2½ wire wheels, 4.75-18 Dunlop Fort tyres **Length** 143in (3632mm) **Wheelbase** 94³⁄₁₆in (2392mm) **Width** 53in (1346mm) **Height** 43in (1092mm) **Front track** 45in (1143mm) **Rear track** 45in (1143mm) **Unladen weight** 1477lb (671kg) **Top speed** Estimated 120mph (193kph)

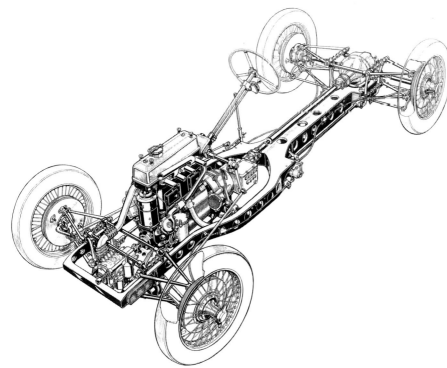

The R-type's Y-shaped chassis with all-independent torsion bar suspension was a remarkable design. Other important features were the larger Zoller supercharger, pre-selector gearbox and centrally mounted steering box with two drop arms.

R-type

As Q-type except: **Brakes** Girling type **Front suspension** Independent with double wishbones and torsion bars, hydraulic shock absorbers **Rear suspension** Independent with double wishbones and torsion bars, hydraulic shock absorbers **Wheels/tyres** Centre-lock 18 × 3 wire wheels, 4.75-18 racing tyres **Length** 141in (3581mm) **Wheelbase** 90.5in (2299mm) **Width** 56.25in (1429mm) **Height** 45in (1143mm) **Front track** 46⅜in (1178mm) **Rear track** 45.5in (1156mm) **Unladen weight** 1388lb (630kg)

TA

Engine In-line four-cylinder **Construction** Cast-iron block and head **Crankshaft** Three main bearings **Bore × stroke** 63.5mm × 102mm (2.5in × 4.016in) **Capacity** 1292cc (78.8cu in) **Valves** Overhead valves operated by push-rods **Compression ratio** 6.5:1 **Fuel system** Two SU semi-downdraught 1¼in carburettors **Maximum power** 50bhp at 4500rpm **Transmission** Four-speed Nuffield-type manual gearbox, synchromesh on third and top from engine no.684 **Final drive ratio** 4.875:1 **Top gear mph per 1000rpm** 16.8mph **Brakes** Lockheed hydraulic working in 9in drums, handbrake mechanical on rear wheels **Front suspension** Beam axle, semi-elliptic springs, Luvax hydraulic lever-arm shock absorbers **Rear suspension** Live axle, semi-elliptic leaf springs, Luvax hydraulic lever-arm shock absorbers **Steering** Bishop Cam, worm and peg type **Wheels/tyres** Centre-lock 19 × 2½ wire wheels, 4.50-19 Dunlop 90 tyres **Length** 139.5in (3543mm) **Wheelbase** 94in (2388mm) **Width** 56in (1422mm) **Height** 53in (1346mm) **Front track** 45in (1143mm) **Rear track** 45in (1143mm) **Unladen weight** Two-seater 1764lb (801kg), drophead coupé 1960lb (890kg) **Top speed** 80mph (129kph) **0-60mph** 23sec **Standing ¼-mile** 22.8sec **Typical fuel consumption** 27-32mpg

TB/TC

As TA except: **Bore × stroke** 66.5mm × 90mm (2.618in × 3.543in) **Capacity** 1250cc (76.28cu in) **Compression ratio** 7.25:1 **Maximum power** 54.4bhp at 5200rpm **Transmission** Synchromesh also on second gear **Final drive ratio** 5.125:1 **Top gear mph per 1000rpm** 15.6mph **Front and rear suspension** Luvax-Girling shock absorbers **Unladen weight** Two-seater 1736lb (788kg) **Top speed** TC: 73-79mph (117-127kph) **0-60mph** TC: 21-23sec **Standing 1/4-mile** TC: 21.8sec **Typical fuel consumption** TC: 28-34mpg

TD

As TB/TC except: **Compression ratio** TD Mark II: 8.1:1, 8.6:1 or 9.2:1 **Fuel system** TD Mark II: 1½in carburettors **Maximum power** TD Mark II: 57-61bhp **Final drive ratio** TD Mark II: 4.875:1, 4.55:1 optional **Top gear mph per 1000rpm** 14.4mph **Front suspension** Independent with wishbones and coil springs, Luvax Girling or later Armstrong hydraulic lever-arm shock absorbers; TD Mark II: additional friction shock absorbers **Rear suspension** Later cars with Armstrong shock absorbers **Steering** Rack and pinion **Wheels/tyres** 15 × 4.00 bolt-on disc wheels, 5.50-15 tyres **Length** 145in (3683mm) **Wheelbase** 94in (2388mm) **Width** 58⅝in (1489mm) **Height** 53in (1346mm) **Front track** 47⅜in (1203mm) **Rear track** 50in (1270mm) **Unladen weight** 1932lb (877kg) **Top speed** 77-83mph (124-134kph), TD Mark II 88mph (142kph) in *Autosport* 29 December 1950, 83mph (134kph) in *Road & Track* 1953 **0-60mph** 21-24sec, TD Mark II 15sec **Standing ¼-mile** 21.5-23.4sec, TD Mark II 20.1sec **Typical fuel consumption** 26-33mpg, TD Mark II 28.5mpg

TF

As TD except: **Compression ratio** 8.1:1 **Fuel system** 1½in carburettors **Maximum power** 57bhp at 5500rpm **Final drive ratio** 4.875:1 **Top gear mph per 1000rpm** 15.2mph **Wheels/tyres** Centre-lock wire wheels optional **Length** 147in (3734mm) **Width** 59⅜in (1518mm) **Height** 52.5in (1334mm) **Front track** With wire wheels 48⅜in (1224mm) **Rear track** With wire wheels 50¹⅜in (1291mm) **Top speed** 80-82mph (129-132kph) **0-60mph** 18.9sec **Standing ¼-mile** 21.6sec **Typical fuel consumption** 24-28mpg

TF 1500

As TF except: **Bore × stroke** 72mm × 90mm (2.835in × 3.543in) **Capacity** 1466cc (89.46cu in) **Compression ratio** 8.3:1 **Maximum power** 63bhp at 5000rpm **Top speed** 85-88mph (137-142kph) **0-60mph** 16.3sec **Standing ¼-mile** 20.7sec **Typical fuel consumption** 28-31mpg

ACKNOWLEDGEMENTS

Grateful thanks are due to the owners whose cars were used for colour photography. Worthy of special mention are Tony and Hilary Newbold, whose TA, TB, TC and TF were photographed specially for this book by John Colley. Neill Bruce provided a large quantity of colour photographs, mainly of pre-war Midgets. Other cars illustrated in colour are owned by Simon Gibbard (TA Tickford), Andrew Nairne (red TD), Malcolm Green (green TD) and the late John Shute (Arnolt-MG). Mike Ellman-Brown kindly made available his superb collection of MG brochures, which were photographed by Tony Baker. Other photographic sources were Geoff Goddard, *Classic and Sportscar* magazine (thanks to Charlie Pierce and Carol Page), *Classic Cars* magazine (thanks to Nick Kisch, Maurice Rowe and Scilla Robinson), British Motor Industry Heritage Trust, Nick Baldwin, David Hodges, Anders Ditlev Clausager, Rinsey Mills and Otis Meyer of *Road & Track* magazine.